LIVES AND EXPLOITS OF THE DARING FRANK AND JESSE JAMES:

Thaddeus Thorndike's Graphic and Realistic Description of Their Many Deeds of Unparalleled Daring in the Robbing of Banks and Railroad Trains

Edited by Don Heinrich Tolzmann

HERITAGE BOOKS, INC.

Other Books By the Author:

Germany and America, 1450-1700
The First Germans in America

Published 1992 By

HERITAGE BOOKS, INC.
1540-E Pointer Ridge Place, Bowie, Maryland 20716
(301)-390-7709

ISBN 1-55613-593-9

A Complete Catalog Listing Hundreds of Titles on
History, Genealogy & Americana
Free on Request

Table of Contents

Preface

The purpose of this work is to make Thaddeus Thorndike's best-seller dealing with the James brothers and their gang again available to the general public. Originally published in 1909, this work has long been out of print. The work is of special interest because it is one of the most popular works dealing with the James Gang. It highlights particularly the lives and exploits of Jesse James (1847-1882) and his elder brother Frank James (1843-1915); although different birth dates are given for the James brothers by Thorndike, the aforementioned are the accepted dates in question.

My interest in Jesse James derives from the fact that for a brief moment in 1876 the path of my grandfather, Albert Tolzmann (1865-1937) of Renville Co., Minnesota, crossed that of the James Gang. It is because of this connection that the editor became interested in Jesse James, and decided to edit this volume for publication.

The assistance of my father, Eckhart H. Tolzmann, not only facilitated this work, but was essential to its completion. A special word of gratitude is in order here to him for having recorded family history, and also for providing me with publications and articles he had collected about the James Gang.

Also, a word of thanks to Professor Barry Thomas, Ohio University, for assistance in locating illustrations used in this work, at the end of Part One, from a volume in the Archives and Special Collections Department, Ohio University Libraries. (1)

DHT

Part One - Editor's Comments

Foreword

Jesse James captured the interest of the American public in the 19th century, and soon became mythologized as an "American Robin Hood." Soon after his death in 1882, he became part of the country's mythology and folklore: the robber-hero. By 1927 there were at least eight silent films dealing with him, and in the following years numerous "talkies" were produced. Even Roy Rogers would play a singing Jesse James. In 1949, President Truman made political use of the James' legend when he said that James had been a modern-day Robin Hood who had stolen from the rich, and given to the poor, which was, in his view, not an entirely bad policy.

More than four hundred books have been written about him, more than one hundred and fifty songs have been recorded about him, and even a rock and roll band in the 1970s took on the name "The James Gang." All of this is an indication not only of the long-lasting public fascination with James, but also the great marketability of anything bearing his and his brother's name.

Why then would a German-American historian take an interest in editing this edition of a work dealing with the James Gang? The answer is best provided in a history of Renville County, Minnesota, published in 1981, which contains the following information about the editor's grandfather, Albert Tolzmann (1865-1937):

"When Albert was still in his teens, the Jesse James brothers and gang were hiding at a neighbor's farm about a mile south from his father's farm in Flora Township. The man and his wife living there were held hostage for about a week while the gang went around stealing horses shortly before their unsuccessful bank robbery at Northfield, Minnesota. Albert got wind of it and put locks on all the barn doors and hid in the hay mow with guns and ammunition. Around midnight he heard someone tampering with the door locks. Quickly he took some shots through a small opening in the wall above the door. That was all that was needed to scare the gang and they speedily fled." (1)

That this was not published until 1981 is not unusual when the following factors are taken into consideration. First, the James Gang, of necessity, often stole horses, especially by tricking the unassuming into believing that they were law enforcement officers. For example, George Huntington reports that after the attempted robbery at Northfield, the gang "stole a fine span of greys, on which they mounted bareback. This capture was a most fortunate one for them, and enabled them to make rapid progress and to assume again the role of officers in pursuit of criminals." (2)

The gang usually "had no difficulty in getting food and information from unsuspecting people, who found only too late how they had been imposed upon." Huntington notes other attempts of the gang to steal horses, and cites a case where they were also fired upon. "The free-booters did not care to risk the encounter, and turning back, took refuge in the river-bottom." (3) Hence, such encounters were not uncommon. Indeed, the gang often attempted to, and many times successfully stole horses - such was their modus operandi. Such events occurred so often, that it is unlikely that they all would have, or could have, been recorded.

A second, and more important reason than the frequent occurrence of such encounters, was the basic reluctance of many to report such incidents. Because both James brothers escaped from Minnesota after the Northfield robbery, it was not considered especially advisable to report on such encounters when they were still alive.

A classic example of this was the case of Oscare Oleson Suborn, a Norwegian-American boy who had assisted in the capture of members of the gang in Minnesota. Interestingly enough, it was not until 1929 that a veterinarian in South Dakota, Dr. Asle Oscar Sorbel, revealed that he had been the Norwegian-American boy who was identified in the press as Suborn.

Why did he wait a full fifty-four years after the Northfield event to report this? Simple. He had adopted this cover name "for fear of reprisals by other gang members and friends of the Missouri outlaws." (4) It should be noted that Jesse lived six years after the robbery, Frank James lived until 1915, and the Younger brothers were released from prison in Minnesota in 1901. Moreover, the "terms of their parole forbade their leaving Minnesota..." (5)

In short, up until the First World War some major members of the gang were still alive, and some of them still in Minnesota. Also, it should be remembered that the Gang had a lot of friends and admirers not only in the home state of Missouri, but elsewhere. Although it is highly unlikely that there was any need to fear reprisals, as did Dr. Sorbel, one can understand an individual's reluctance to mention encounters with the James Gang.

Third, if these two factors did not encourage reticence, then certainly the great mass popularity of the James brothers might have. What would be the point of reporting a relatively common encounter with a gang, many of whose members were not only still alive, but were immensely popular with the public at large?

Indeed, the James Gang was so popular that the "Cole Younger and Frank James Historical Wild West Show" was launched in the early 1900s. Although Frank James retired from the show by World War I, Younger continued until his death in 1916.

"Long before the deaths of Cole and Frank, Jesse James had been enshrined in the pantheon of American popular heroes, and the exploits of Jesse, Frank, and Cole had become raw material for virtually all forms of popular entertainment, from dime novels to stage plays." (6) Since 1948, Northfield, Minnesota, has staged popular re-enactments of the famous robbery there, "The Defeat of Jesse James Days," an event which annually attracts fifty thousand people. (7)

Finally, a linguistic matter to take into consideration is that at the time of the robbery my grandfather spoke little, or no English. His parents were German immigrants and they lived in a German-speaking community. My grandfather never attended public schools and was entirely educated at home. His son, my father (born 1904), was also raised in a German-speaking family, and learned English as a foreign language when he began attending the public school. And I also learned German in my family. The point here is that, my grandfather's youthful experience probably was only communicated in his family and within the local German-American community. By the 1930s, the whole experience was nothing more than an anecdote to my grandfather, but nevertheless one which he took an interest in telling.

All of the above factors most likely contributed to the fact that my grandfather said little outside of the Tolzmann family and the German-American community in Renville County about his youthful encounter with Jesse James. In any event, it remained a well-known aspect of Tolzmann family history, so that only in 1981 did my father, Eckhart H. Tolzmann, choose to report the event to the Renville

County Historical Society, which was at that time compiling its history. (8)

My family and relatives have always known about the encounter of my grandfather with the James Gang, and have, therefore, always been interested in the history of the James brothers.

Indeed, there was always a great sense of pride in my grandfather who had stood guard at the family farm when he was only a youth - his heroic act in the face of an attempted robbery had protected home and family. Had it not been for this coincidental connection with the James Gang, the editor, as well as his family, may not have had more than a general interest in the James Gang. Indeed, a Confederate guerrilla/highwayman has little in common with a German farming family.

However, because the James Gang came to Minnesota, they of necessity intruded and imposed themselves into the lives and family histories of many people. Why did all of this happen and what is the history of the James Gang, are questions the editor has often heard. For this reason, as well as in special honor of his grandfather, Albert Tolzmann, the editor chose to edit a work long in the possession of his family.

Albert Tolzmann stood guard in the hay mow of this log-barn, now covered with siding, which was built in 1871. It is located in Renville County, Flora Township, Section 34.

The vault at the First National Bank of Northfield

Introduction

Jesse Woodson James was born 5 September 1847 near Kearney, Clay County, Missouri. His brother, Alexander Franklin, was born 10 January 1843 in Scott County, Kentucky. Their parents, Robert and Zerelda (Cole) James, were Kentuckians who had moved west to Missouri after their marriage. The father, a Baptist minister, supported himself by farming. In 1851, he traveled to California, where he passed away. Mrs. James married again, but then was divorced, and in 1855 married Dr. Reuben Samuels, a physician and farmer.

Both Jesse and Frank James received little formal education, but on the farm received a religious education and were considered to be "good boys," and Jesse was said to have remained a "devout Christian" his whole life. As a result of the pro-Southern sympathies of the family, the farm was raided twice in the Civil War by Federal troops, and "suffered greatly at the hands of Union forces." (1)

In retaliation, Jesse became an informer, and then both he and his brother joined the Confederate guerrillas, known as Quantrill's Raiders. Jesse joined at the age of 15, and soon acquired a reputation for his daring and marksmanship. Frank left Quantrill in 1864 and joined forces with "Bloody Bill" Anderson, whom Jesse also joined at age 17. When the Civil War came to an end in 1865, James and others surrendered, but he "was treacherously shot and severely wounded." It took about a year for him to recover from his wounds. Perhaps it could be said that the Civil War never really came to an end for the James Boys. Indeed, it was said that the Civil War had made them Confederate guerrillas. It was in 1866 that Coleman Younger and others formed "a band of brigands" of which Jesse became the leader, and would lead for the next fifteen years or so. On 13 February 1866, the group robbed the Clay County Savings Bank of $60,000 - the first peacetime bank robbery during daytime in American history. The James' associates, the Youngers, consisted of four brothers: Cole, who had been one of Quantrill's lieutenants, James, Bob, and John. Over the course of time, about fourteen individuals were known to have been members of the gang. From 1866 on, Jesse James was declared an outlaw, and remained so until his death.

The James Gang "specialized in bank robberies, but on July 21, 1873, initiated a novel enterprise by holding up and robbing a train on the Rock Island railroad at Adir, Iowa." After this, lucrative rewards began to be offered for the apprehension of the James Gang, and by 1874 the Pinkerton detectives began to scrutinize the Gang closely. Also, after 1873/74, the Gang became forever associated with bank and train robberies, which one source even went so far as to describe as having been "accomplished with artistry and sucess." Also, after each robbery which was ascribed to Jesse, he "customarily published a letter proclaiming his innocence and establishing an alibi." To add to the confusion, he would write press releases about robberies that had not occurred, send them to newspapers, and then later proceed to do what he had written about. It is an understatement that with the James Gang we are talking about a fairly intelligent and well-organized group. It was said that Jesse was "chivalrous to women and good to the old and poor." After one robbery, a professor stated that if he had to be robbed, he preferred to have been robbed by a "first-class" robber with a national reputation. It is, therefore, not surprising that he soon acquired "a Robin Hood reputation among the people of his region." Eventually, he came to be described as an "American outlaw of the Robin Hood type," since some considered him "daring and colorful." (2)

The James boys were noted for being audacious and impudent. One of their robberies took place during a political rally - before it was over Jesse rode up to the gathering and announced that he thought someone had robbed the bank. On another occasion he robbed the cash box at the Kansas City Fair which was attended by ten thousand people. These exploits only added to the reputation of the James Boys.

It should be noted that James attacked public institutions, which many disliked after the Civil War: railroads and banks. Some viewed him as representing the common folk against big business. Some no doubt saw him as a Confederate hero. All of this contributed to the legend in the making. It is also thought that he followed the newspapers and what the image was that was developing of him, and acted accordingly. There is no question that he understood public relations.

Public sympathy for the gang on a large scale came dramatically in 1875 as a result of a raid on the family farm by Pinkerton detectives. When it happened, "it served to win the James boys the sympathy of many people..." (3) On 26 January 1875, Dr. and Mrs. Samuels were suddenly awakened to discover "a ball of cotton, saturated with some flammable substance, blazing in their kitchen." As they removed this to the fireplace, another one was then thrown through a window. This was also placed in the fireplace where it exploded with a tremendous impact. A large fragment of the bomb struck Archie Peyton Samuels, the nine-year-old half-brother of Frank and Jesse, and killed him. Their mother's "right hand was mangled so badly that amputation was necessary..." Moreover, a servant was also wounded. Regardless of the charges against the James brothers, "the murder of an innocent child and the maiming of their mother by law officers outraged people everywhere." (4)

Newspapers immediately condemned the brutal act, stating, for example, that "the James boys never fired a dwelling at midnight." Another newspaper in Kansas City stated, "There is no crime, however dastardly, which merits a retribution as savage and fiendish as the one which these men acting under the semblance of law have perpetrated." (5)

The next year found the James Gang in Minnesota where they attempted to rob the bank at Northfield. It had been reported that General Benjamin Butler of

Massachusetts and his son-in-law, J.T. Ames, had desposited large amounts of money there. Due to Butler's harsh treatment of Southerners in the Civil War, "the attempted robbery took on the stature of a raid by the South against the North and reinforced the legend of the outlaws as Southern patriots." (6) At least, this was the rationalization later offered by Cole Younger for the reason the gang traveled north to Minnesota. Another factor to take into consideration was that a member of the gang, William Stiles, was from Minnesota.

The attempted robbery on 7 September 1876 was a disaster which resulted in losing six of the eight members of the gang (three were killed and the following three were captured: Cole, Robert, and James Younger) - only Frank and Jesse James escaped.

For three years, they remained in retirement and seclusion, but in 1879, with a new group, they robbed a train, and in 1881, two more trains. However, time was running out.

In 1881, William H. Wallace was elected as prosecuting attorney of Jackson County, Missouri, and he stood for a platform demanding the arrest of the outlaws which "marked a change in the local sentiment that had protected them and the beginning of a relentless prosecution." (7)

The new prosecution led to the arrest and conviction of three members of the gang. Another gave himself up after killing a fellow gang member. Then another was killed by Jesse James based on suspicion that he had been unfaithful to the group.

After robbing a Chicago & Alton train at Blue Cut, Missouri, in September 1881, Jesse shook hands with the conductor, and said: "You'll never hear from me again." He apparently planned to abandon the life he had been leading, and move west to a farm in Nebraska with his wife and two children, but he would never make it.

In the spring of 1882 Jesse James was shot by a member of his band, Robert Ford, and fatally wounded. "Jesse's grief-stricken wife rushed to his side, and townspeople swarmed to the house to view the notorious outlaw's body." James had been living as Mr. Thomas Howard at St. Joseph, Missouri, for almost six months. His killer became immediately known nationally as that "dirty little coward" for having shot James in the back of the head. He apparently had arranged a deal with Missouri Governor Crittenden to obtain the reward ($5,000) for the capture of James dead or alive. Jesse James' assassination "at the hands of a traitor, followed by widely reported scenes of his grieving widow and children, became the final indispensable elements in the hero-making process." An ardent supporter of James, John Edwards, editor of the *Sedalia Democrat*, wrote, "Such a cry of horror and indignation is thundering over the land" that if the assassin "had either manhood, conscience or courage, he would go, as another Judas, and hang himself." Later, it was claimed that James "never desired to be a fugitive and many times would have given himself up, had he been assured of protection and a fair trial." Some also claimed that it was the historical circumstances of his background which had contributed to the course his life had taken. (8)

In the time the Gang existed, it had made off with an estimated total of a half-million dollars, which in the nineteenth century cleary was a fortune. However, the price was high - the number of deaths incurred was thirty-two, including fifteen members of the Gang and four Pinkerton agents.

The long career of the Gang was partially due to the elaborate preparation and espionage undertaken by Frank and Jesse - they knew the escape routes, the lawmen, the landscape, the people, etc. Also, in addition they had been so well liked by so many for such a long time.

The making of the legend of Jesse James, however, had already begun before his death. In early 1882 a book by D.W. Stevens was published, which drew strong parallels between Jesse James and Robin Hood. In the 1880s/90s numerous dime novels appeared about the James Gang, and in 1895 George Huntington published his *Robber and Hero: The Story of the Northfield Bank Raid*. (9) Many, many books have been published ever since that time, down to the present, with no apparent abatement in the fascination and interest with the James brothers and their gang.

John McGuigan notes that the real question regarding this fascination is "What's the meaning of Jesse James?" He cites Stephen Tatum's analysis of outlaw-heroes of the American Wild West. Tatum claims that there is a dialectic of success and failure related to the basic human need "for an intensely exciting, unpredictable world and for an ordered, secure, routine world." Some may see these needs fulfilled in the lives and exploits of the James brothers. Also, the outlaw fulfills the need and desire to belong to a band, club, or group. However, the outlaw must ultimately perish, so that the community can exist. In defeat, however, the outlaw becomes a hero. There is safety for the community in the defeat of the outlaw, who then "becomes removed safely into the legend of the past." (10)

Another interesting comment the editor came upon was found in a book of reminiscences by a member of the Quantrill raiders who knew Jesse James. He felt that James' life had basically been molded by the historical circumstances of the time. He asked "Dear Reader, what would you have done under the same circumstances? Put yourselves in the Jameses' and Youngers' places, and think it over." (11)

Confederate sympathizers obviously saw in Jesse James a hero of a lost cause. Others may have sympathized with James as an apparent "underdog" whom fate had dealt a "raw deal." And others may be attracted by the legends surrounding Jesse James as the "American Robin Hood," legends created in part by numerous books and by Hollywood. Another factor is that Jesse James touched on the lives of many people from Missouri to Minnesota. Adding to the popularity of Jesse James, no doubt, are the tragic aspects associated with his life and death, which first brought forth waves of sympathy from the public when they happened.

William Settle notes that "the Jesse James legend will live on and continue to excite Americans with the exploits of their native Robin Hood." (12) John McGuigan notes that "each generation creates its own meaning, depending upon shifts of social and cultural mood and historical circumstances." (13)

The aforementioned factors undoubtedly contribute to the interest in James, but there are perhaps a number of general factors also at play. The fascination in James may also be part of the general interest in the era of the Wild West - roughly the latter third of the nineteenth century. This period definitely saw the end of an era. As the century moved on the Wild West and its frontier days were brought to a close with the arrival of the settlers and the immigrants. Indeed the advancing frontier ultimately brought an end to the Wild West. However, there always remained an interest in representatives of that bygone era.

Perhaps this interest is indicative of interest in the American frontier past, and there were many other fascinating characters, aside from James, on both sides of the law. On one side there was Billy the Kid,

John Wesley Harding, the Daltons etc., and on the other side were men like Wild Bill Hickock, Wyatt Earp, etc. In some cases, there was even a considerable gray area between the so-called "good" and "bad" guys. (14) All of them, however, belonged to the passing era of the Wild West. In conclusion, it should be said that those who want to understand the James Brothers should take a closer look not only at their lives, but also the times in which they lived during and after the Civil War, the bygone era of the Wild West

yours respectfully
Zerelda Samuel.

(Formerly Mrs. James,) Mother of Frank and Jesse James.

DR. REUBEN SAMUEL.

Step-father of Frank and Jesse James.

FRANK AND JESSE JAMES.

A Narrow Escape.

Part Two - Thorndike's Description

LIVES AND EXPLOITS

OF THE DARING

FRANK AND JESSE JAMES

CONTAINING

A GRAPHIC AND REALISTIC DESCRIPTION OF THEIR MANY
DEEDS OF UNPARALLELED DARING IN THE ROB-
BING OF BANKS AND RAILROAD TRAINS.

BY

THADDEUS THORNDIKE

I. & M. OTTENHEIMER, PUBLISHERS,
321 WEST BALTIMORE STREET,
BALTIMORE, MD.

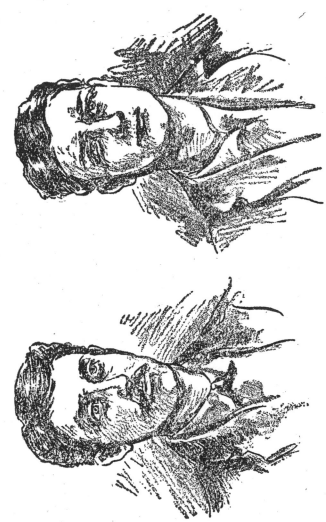

Frank and Jesse James when they were members of the famous Quantrell Guerrillas.

CONTENTS.

v

CONTENTS—Continued.

vi

Lives and Exploits of the Daring Frank and Jesse James

CHAPTER I.

EARLY HISTORY OF THE JAMES BOYS.

Frank James was born in Scott county, Kentucky, in 1841; and Jesse in Clay county, Missouri, in 1845. The father of the two boys was a Baptist preacher in Missouri, and when Jesse was only five years old his father was seized with the prevailing gold fever, and, leaving wife and children on the home farm, migrated to that Eldorado—Colifornia—and was there stricken down by a mortal disease and died.

Seven years after the minister's demise the widow became the wife of Dr. Reuben Samuels, of Kentucky.

In 1861-2—When the outspoken secession proclivities of the family caused them to be suspected of affording "aid and comfort" to the enemy, the loyalists came down on the farm, hung Dr. Samuels long enough to choke him into insensibility, from which unpleasant situation he was cut down and resuscitated by his devoted spouse. Previous to this Frank James had joined the notorious guerrilla leader, Quantrell. Young Jesse, finding the country too hot for him, joined his brother, and the two, under the command of Quantrell, helped to make the bloody history of civil war in Kansas and Missouri.

One of the closing episodes of this terrible guerrilla warfare, in which the elder brother, Frank, took part, is related as follows:

On the 4th of December, 1864, Quantrell gathered his last command about him and started on his last pilgrimage of butchery. The old fire was dying down and the fearless bandit of the hills was but a shadow of his former self. But if the old tiger is less lithe and active, its growl is just as savage and its taste for blood as keen. Many of Quantrell's most valiant and trusted comrades have died a death as awful as their lives had been—remorseless and cruel. Quantrell gathered about him between thirty and forty guerrillas, and with Frank James as a sort of lieutenant, the band started for Kentucky. The Confederate armies had retreated from Missouri, and Quantrell felt that Kentucky would afford a fairer field for his pur poses than Missouri. So, in the very beginning ot a hard winter, they left Wigginton for Kentucky. They went in the teeth of difficulties of all sorts, raiding and pillaging and murdering in the summer months—when the woods form a grateful shelter and the brushwood serves for a bed and the camp-fire gleams romantic-ally—is one thing; but the pursuit of such a perilous career in the teeth of winter is another. And this was not all. The militiamen had sworn by every oath that was binding to have Quantrell's life. It was only a question of time. The dread warrior's days were numbered. It was with difficulty he and his fol-lowers succeeded in getting out of Missouri alive. They were pursued hard by Captain Curtis and his troops on to the Arkansas line, but there the trail was lost, and the desperadoes crossed into Kentucky. On New Year's Day, 1865, they crossed the Mississippi River at Pacific Place, about sixteen miles above Mem-phis. They marched on through Big Creek, Covington, Tabernack, Humboldt, Milan and on to Paris. From thence to Birmingham; pressing forward, they crossed the Tennessee River and went through Canton and Cadiz to a place called Hopkinsville. Here they had an adventure of some interest. Stray shots by the way had resulted in one or two scattered murders per diem, but there had been nothing to satisfy the greed of a guerrilla.

Arrived at Hopkinsville, they found a house in which twelve cavalrymen were taking their leisure. But on the first token of their coming, nine out of the twelve military heroes manifested that discretion which is the better part of valor and made themselves *non est inventus*. But the remaining three determined to fight to the bitter end. It was a fight against great odds— three to thirty-five. Three but poorly equipped soldiers against thirty-five merciless guerrillas! The gallant three blockaded the house, and held out for hours, answering back the challenge to surrender with such ammunition as they possessed. At last Frank James told them that if they did not surrender, he should be compelled to burn their stronghold; and it was not till the house was burning about their ears that these poor wretches, half scorched, half suffocated, rushed through the flames to meet instant death from the deliberate, well-aimed shots of their relentless foes. They took the twelve horses the soldiers had left as spoils of war. So closed another day of robbery, fire and murder. The chief spirit of this fray was Frank James.

At Hartford, in Ohio county, he played the role of a Federal captain and described his band as a **Federal** troop in hot pursuit of bloodthirty guerrillas. So successfully was the deception carried out that he thoroughly imposed upon the credulity of Capt. Frank Barnette, the captain of a company of Kentucky Federal militamen. Barnette and Quantrell became firm friends, and it was not long before Barnette was persuaded by the wily bandit to go on an expedition to hunt for Confederate guerrillas. Barnette and his company, little dreaming of the sad doom that awaited them, rode out.

Quantrell had given orders that every man would be assassinated. He had arranged the plan of slaughter. His men were to ride beside the Federal soldiers; he was at an opportune moment to draw his pocket-handkerchief carelessly from his pocket and throw it over his shoulder. That was to be the sign for slaughter—quick and complete. The unsuspecting Federals rode on. About five o'clock in the afternoon, just as the winter's sun was sinking behind the western hills, they reached a stream of water at a ford. The fatal sign was given. Quick as thought Frank James sent a bullet through the gallant heart of Captain Barnette, who fell dead from his horse without a single groan, his blood curdling in the blue waters beneath. Every man shot his man, while Quantrell from a hollow tree watched with fiendish complacency the ruthless murder of the whole Federal troop.

It will not be surprising that this last dark deed of violence, in which the most shameless treachery played so large a part, awoke the ungovernable anger of the Federal soldiers, whose compatriots in arms had been so mercilessly destroyed. They were determined to hunt Quantrell to the death; and they did not fail of their purpose. They drove the wild tiger of the black flag from lair to lair, from hiding-place to hiding-place, until at last within a few days after the dastardly outrage of Hartford, Major Bridgewater and Captain Farrell, with a large Federal following, confronted Quantrell and his band in their last stronghold. It was Quantrell's last fight. Strangely enough Frank James was not in this last fray; he had been away on a visit, and was not with his chieftain when he fell, for which he never forgave himself. The soldiers drove Quantrell and his now diminished band of guerrillas into a village called Smiley. Here, finding escape utterly impossible, being hemmed in on every side, Quantrell made his last stand. It was an awful fight—a fight intended to be one of utter extermination. There were three hundred against forty! Gashed and wounded and covered with blood and dust,

Frank James rode leisurely into Brandenburg.

Quantrell fought on, till blinded with his own blood, riddled through and through with a score of bullets, he fell at last mortally wounded, with an empty pistol in one hand and a sword reeking with blood in the other.

So fell the scourge and curse of Missouri.

Frank James gave his parole at Samuel's Depot, Nelson county, Kentucky, July 25th, 1865. Yet he did not at once return to his native State. He was in point of fact an exile from Missouri, and for some time he lingered in Kentucky.

About this time he was passing from Nelson county to Brandenburg, in Meade county, on the Ohio River. He was not aware that Brandenburg was the favored rendezvous of horse thieves, nor that a very large number of valuable horses had just been stolen from La Rue. Such, however, was the case. The people were up in arms against the thieves, and a number of disbanded Federals were now busy chasing these idle robbers. Frank James, alike ignorant and innocent, rode leisurely into Brandenburg and sought the quiet of the hotel. He was sitting quietly in the hotel, without the slightest dream of trouble, when a posse of four men, with a magnificent giant of a man at their head, entered. Whether they had been informed that

Frank James, the noted guerrilla, was at the inn is not known. The leader of the company laid his hand on Frank's shoulder and said mildly and half-pleasantly:

"I arrest you as a horse thief!"

Frank took in the whole situation in a moment. But moved no muscle, betrayed no sign. He, of course, was not unarmed. The leader of the four saw only in his prisoner a young fellow of two and twenty, a little bronzed and travel-stained; there was nothing to alarm him in the clear gaze of young Frank.

"You will consider yourself under arrest," added the speaker.

"I consider no such proposition," said Frank, and as he spoke his hands went to his belt, and before the arresting party as much as noticed the movement, two of them lay at Frank's feet, shot dead by his revolvers that never failed him; a third was writhing in mortal agony and the fourth was fleeing for his life. As he fled, however, he fired a parting shot, which nearly cost Frank his life. It made a terrible wound in his left hip, which rendered him almost unable to move. But his blood was roused. The old guerrilla spirit flamed up again. The wildest excitement ensued, there was instantly a crowd gathered round the hotel, and the forms of the men bespoke an angry purpose; but

Frank, ever dauntless, crawled to a post near at hand, and, though they cursed and threatened, he ordered them on peril of their lives to stand back, and they obeyed.

In the midst of all this excitement some daring young spirit, who had known Frank in other days, dashed through the noisy crowd and half-helped, half-dragged Frank on to his horse and rode away with him, and not one of all the valiant Brandenburgers attempted for one moment to arrest or stay the departure of this man, who had wrought a triple murder in their sight.

Frank's preserver drove him away to a safe hiding place and procured him the most skilful medical assistance. The ghastly wound brought him to the door of death, and whole weeks passed away before the doctor pronounced him out of danger. But months of suffering followed. Indeed, years after Frank declared that he felt the effects of the shot of "that damnable Brandenburger."

During his months of enforced quiet he brooded over his lot and felt that it was utterly vain for him to dream of any peaceful way of life. The die was cast. What was the odds? He had good luck and bad luck. One thing was pretty clear to him—he would have to fight life out on the line he had voluntarily selected.

CHAPTER II.

THE RUSSELLVILLE BANK ROBBERY.

While Frank James was in hiding and nursing his wound Jesse was at the family home in Clay county, Missouri, slowly recovering from a gun shot wound through the left lung.

On February 14, 1866, a great robbery took place at Liberty, Mo., that aroused the greatest excitement through all that Western district. The Commercial Bank, of Liberty, was robbed of a sum of money close upon $70,000. The names of the James boys were immediately connected with the robbery. And yet there were many who still believed that they were honest men. Jesse had but recently returned from Nebraska, and was still weak and suffering, and could hardly have had any direct hand in the robbery. Still the almost universal opinion was that he had planned the robbery. And, indeed, it was believed that a good share of the booty secured from the bank found its way to Frank and Jesse James

However this may be, a company of men, who were stinging from old wounds, determined to put an end to Jesse's depredations by quietly handing him over to the civil power. And so four days after the bank robbery at Liberty they matured their plans. They had no desire to kill Jesse, only to secure him and imprison him. Accordingly close on the hour of midnight of February 18th, 1866, six well armed, well-mounted militia men rode up to the home of Dr. Samuels. Jesse was suffering from a burning fever and was tossing from side to side, when his quick ear detected the sounds of horses' hoofs crunching the crisp winter snow. In a moment he was on the alert. His two trusty companions—his revolvers—were under his pillow loaded. The heavy tramp of five men was soon heard coming along the piazza, and, knocking at the door with the butt end of their guns, they demanded immediate admission.

Dr. Samuels gained a little time by parleying at the door, telling these midnight visitors to "be patient a moment, there was something wrong with the blamed lock." Meantime Jesse, looking through the window and taking in the whole situation, crawled down to the foot of the stairs.

"What shall I do?" whispered the doctor. "Open

the door the moment I tell you," Jesse answered in a faint voice, looking carefully at his weapons of defense. The besiegers grew impatient, and, amid muttered curses on the whole family, began to beat in the panels of the door with guns, demanding that "that murdering thief, Jesse, should come and surrender at once," declaring they would take him either dead or alive. Jesse was ready with the answer. But the answer they got was a fearful one. The door opened, and, standing half-hidden in the shadow of the doorway, Jesse fired with unerring precision, and two of the company fell instantly dead, staining the virgin snow with the crimson torrents of their heart's blood.

Standing now full in the doorway, the moonlight falling on his pale, spectral face, and before the report of his first shots had fully died away, he fired again, and two more of the squad fell, writhing in agony and pain. The rest of that blustering, blasphemous company fled to their horses and rode away in the moonlight, leaving behind their dead and dying comrades.

Weak and feeble as he was, Jesse was wide awake to his peril. The escaped soldiers would bear the tidings of the midnight slaughter to the people all around. It would be foolish to wait and try conclusions with a largely augmented force; so Jesse, weak as he was, mounted his horse and rode rapidly away.

The news of this last relentless massacre spread like wildfire. Wearied and worn with the frightful experiences of four years of civil strife, the Missourians longed for peace. They did not stop to ask how this last fray at the Samuels' homestead commenced. Only the dreadful fact that Jesse had killed and wounded four out of six of these soldiers, and had driven the others away in dread alarm, was present to the minds of the people of the neighborhood. A spirit of grave and awful determination arose amongst them. Jesse James must die! Frank was absent. Where, they knew not, nor cared. But here was Jesse; and if of the two one was more daring, more deliberate, more cold-blooded than the other, surely it was Jesse. A large crowd, fifty strong, well armed, sought the Kearney farm and demanded that Jesse should be delivered to them. They swore a solemn oath that they would take him, dead or alive.

So the hunt was up for Jesse James, but it was in in vain. All the most solemn asseverations of Dr. Samuels were regarded as so many subterfuges to gain time. The woods, the farms, the barns, the stables, all were searched, but searched in vain.

The tragedy at Brandenburg and this last fray of

Jesse's did much to settle the future of the James brothers However much they might be disposed to return to a quiet life, circumstances seemed all against them. Men and women everywhere were as much afraid of them as they were ashamed of them. And the general belief was that these awful fires that burned in the hearts of the young bandits were by no means quenched; only smothered for a time, and that at the first excuse they would flame up again blood red. So it came to pass that anything that occurred of an unusually desperate character was quietly and without much inquiry laid to the door of Frank and Jesse James. They had won such a reputation that nothing they could do was thought worse than they had done. So that if horses are stolen at La Rue, or a bank is robbed at Liberty, then, of course, Frank is a horse-thief and Jesse is a bank-robber. And they are at once condemned in the public mind without judge or jury or any very long consideration. One need not wonder very much, then, that, talking the whole matter over one day, Jesse, ever the more talkative of the two, would break forth with this piece of fool's philosophy: "See, Frank, it's no use fighting against all this d——d prejudice; we've got the name anyway; we might as well have the *game and the name* as the name *without* the game."

"All right," said Frank, in his usual surly manner, "go ahead, and the devil take the hindermost."

The pistol shots at Lexington and Brandenburg had very seriously wounded both the robbers. Frank had to stay for some time with friends in Kentucky. After the eventful moonlight night at Kearney, Jesse made his way slowly and most stealthily to Nelson county, Kentucky. There he found Frank. Jesse's long and perilous ride from Kearney had been exceedingly trying. It was not till early in the following year (1868) that Jesse became thoroughly convalescent.

But the one question in many forms was present to the minds of Frank and Jesse, and if Frank spoke of it less frequently than Jesse, it was not because he thought less of it. What was their future to be? The gateways of ordinary careers were closed against them; and, besides all this, they began more and more to realize the terrible strain of inaction. Resting quietly upon your oars is all very well for a little time, but to an active, energetic mind enforced inaction is terrible to endure. What was to be done? The war was over, and there was no military occupation for them. Besides, they were the followers of a fallen cause. Slowly but surely there dawned upon them the possible career of plunder. Should the murderers turn robbers? They never asked this question boldly and plainly, but in some shape or another, vaguely, but not less certainly, the question was pressing itself home upon them. Many of the friends of Jesse James, while they would not openly aver that he was concerned in the Liberty bank robbery, did not scruple to hint that some of the funds of the bank were sustaining both the brothers during their prolonged and perilous sickness. Should they start forth on a career of plunder? Up to this time their characters for honesty had never been impeached. Indeed, many of the bitterest foes of the James brothers held them in a kind of respect. At least they had universal credit for these three points of character: All Missouri said that the Jameses were: First, as true as steel to their friends and comrades; next, they were always courteous and respectful to women; and, lastly, they were as honest as the day. Were they to throw away this last clause of character? Were the murderers to become robbers? That was the question.

To what extent Frank and Jesse and their friends had become organized is not known. For a time, at least, they were forming plans in secret. At last the Western world became aware that they had not been wholly inactive. The sense of security which was spreading throughout the country was most suddenly disturbed.

Russelville—the next scene of their exploits—is a pleasant little village of three to four thousands inhabitants. It is most pleasantly situated in Logan county, on the southern frontier, adjoining Tennessee. It is quite a centre of a large, thriving agricultural district. And its bank became in consequence the depository of a good deal of wealth.

It was a beautiful spring morning. The stores were open and the store-dealers were beginning their business for the day. Now and then a rumbling wagon, corn laden, creaked along the quiet street. The bank was just about to open its doors, when suddenly a clatter of hoofs was heard. Sharp, quick and terrible as the crash of doom, a dozen horsemen, each armed with two pairs of revolvers, dashed down the street, to the terror and amazement of the villagers. With the most fearful oaths and threatenings these armed brigands commanded the people to go into their houses and keep quiet on pain of instant death, and to confirm their purpose they fired in all directions. Two of the men—of whom Jesse James was one and Cole Younger the other—dismounted at the bank and entered. The cashier had opened the safe and the books were out on the counters, and a quantity of gold was spread out before the cashier, which he was then in the act of counting. The sudden entrance of these armed men astonished him for a moment. He turned at once to the safe and was in the act of swinging back the door, when Jesse James said:

"Leave that alone and keep quiet, or I'll blow your brains out."

What could the cashier do with such a threat in his ears, supported as it was by the loaded revolvers too close to said brains to be pleasant? The cashier, setting a higher value on his life than all the gold in the safe, kept quiet, and the safe was rifled. The loose gold on the counter was swept off by Cole Younger. Everything of value was taken away except a few revenue and postage stamps. These the robbers thought hardly worth the trouble of taking, and so Jesse, to whom a joke was never untimely, tossed back the stamps, remarking to the affrighted cashier that he "might want to mail letters later in the day!"

The booty secured, the robbers departed as they came, cursing and threatening instant death to any who dared to follow. No one blamed the cashier of the bank. He was thoroughly helpless. The safe was open, and all he could have done would have been to throw away his life without saving a penny to the bank. The amount stolen has been variously estimated, but all told there could not have been much less than $100,000, which sum, divided between ten men, would make a pretty considerable fortune for each man.

The leaders of the raid were Jesse James, Cole Younger, Jim White, George and Oll. Shepherd; and if Frank James had no active part in the robbery, he probably had his share, and a very good share, in arranging and planning the whole affair.

After the first surprise of the daring robbery had passed away, it was resolved to make a most determined and exhaustive pursuit. The pursuit was long, untiring, but fruitless. The blood of the Kentuckians was up, but it was all in vain. The scent became fainter and fainter, till at last, utterly worn out and dispirited, they returned home, their expedition having utterly failed. George Shepherd, however, was subsequently arrested. He was convicted and sent to the penitentiary for a term of years.

Only one other member of that robber gang was ever found, and that was Oll. Shepherd. He was found in Jackson county, Missouri. A warrant for arrest was issued, but Oll declared he would never be

"Never! Death before surrender."

arrested. A body of from twelve to twenty men were detailed for his arrest. They surrounded him, well armed, and called out to him:

"Surrender or die! Which shall it be? Will you surrender?"

"Never! Death before surrender a thousand times! Do your worst!" shouted the valiant old guerrilla.

Then the awful work began. Shots came thick and fast. It could only be a question of a little time, but Oll Shepherd fought to the last. He stood with his back to a tree and emptied his revolver, firing fourteen shots in wild despair. At last he reeled and staggered, but it was not till his body had received seven bullets that he fell—fell like the old Greek warrior, fighting with death to the last!

Every other member of that robber band that wrought such consternation in Russelville that bright spring morning escaped.

The James boys parted company for a while, but they both set their faces toward San Francisco.

Frank and Jesse met at last at the home of their uncle, Mr. D. W. James, who was then proprietor of the Paso Robel Hot Sulphur Springs. Here the brothers spent a calm and peaceful life for months.

Through the whole summer of 1869 the brothers lived without a single adventure, save the very desirable change from weakness to robust health.

CHAPTER III.

SHAKING UP A CAMP.

At this time the mining camps of Nevada were the homes of wild romance. Frank and Jesse took a journey up the mountains without any special purpose other than that of seeing the country. Of course, they were not likely to risk their lives among the miners of the Sierras unarmed. So, carrying with them their weapons of defense—their faithful companions of the days of peril—they started forth. The camp life was most congenial to them. And, to add to their pleasure, they found several old companions who had followed the black flag of Qauntrell in the old days. They prospected, they played sportsmen, till little by little the old fires were kindling, and there needed only some circumstance to set the old guerrilla flame aglow.

The occasion was not far to seek. Frank and Jesse, with two old Missourian acquaintances, took a journey into the region of the Sonoma Mountains, where a small tributary of the Humboldt River cuts the foot-

hills of the range. There was a new encampment
called "Battle Mountain." And, to use the emphatic
language of these four Missouri boys, they thought
they would break the monotony of life by going to
Battle Mountain "just to shake up the encampment!"
These camping towns spring up as if by magic. And
very often just as rapidly pass from sight. Some
lucky "find" would determine the locality. A main
street would be laid out. Saloons, eating-houses,
dance-houses and gambling-hells, with a sufficient
number of shanties for the dwelling of men, would
make up the "place." And, over and over again, the
gold for which men had toiled so hard for weeks
would be squandered in a single night's debauch.
Battle Mountain had the reputation of being a "rat-
tling place." It had among its strange inhabitants
men of honorable position, charmed by the hope of
finding sudden wealth; and men of easy mind and
careless mien, who were simply traveling to see what
was to be seen, and others of dark intent, who knew
best of all how to gamble and carouse, one of their
chief amusements being to make tenderfeet dance to
avoid the bullets which were fired in unpleasant
proximity to their toes. They were always ready
with bowie knife and revolver as the quick

and sure settlers of any argument that might arise. Hard work by day, and at night women, whiskey and cards; this was the order of Battle Mountain. And it was to "shake up" this encampment that Frank and Jesse James and their two companions from Missouri came. They had not been here long when a number of gallant blacklegs, who little knew what sort of men they had to deal with, formed a plot to swindle these green boys from Missouri. While the James boys did not drink, they were somewhat proud of their skill at cards. One fatal night the boys of Battle Mountain, thirty or forty strong, were gathered together. Some were drinking, others playing at cards, others mapping out plans for future prospceting.

Jesse's friend, sitting at the same table, had just "called" the hand of his oppor nt, one of the men in the plot.

"Three kings," said the gambler, cheerfully.

"Three aces," coolly replied the other, as he exhibited them and raked down the "pot." Then he continued: "I discarded a king. When the cut was made for your deal, the bottom card was exposed. It was a *king*. You got your third king from the bottom. You musn't do that again."

"It's a lie!" snarled the gambler through clenched

One of their chief amusements being to make tenderfeet dance.

teeth. And there was a look in his steel-gray eyes that meant mischief, as his hand felt down for his revolver.

The attention of the whole company was arrested. Jesse took in the whole situation in a moment. His companion had made a deliberate charge of cheating, and Jesse knew well that according to the gamblers' code of honor in such a case "some one must die." There was a moment of peril for his friend, but quick as thought Jesse's pistol flashed its unerring fire, and the gambler cheat fell dead.

The remaining gambler made a lunge at Jesse with a knife. The blow was partly warded off by a tough buckskin bag of gold dust which Jesse carried. The next moment Jesse brought his pistol round with a swing, fired, and literally blew off the top of his opponent's head, and he fell with his face downwards upon the gambling table.

A perfect pandemonium ensued. Frank and his companion were ready for action in a moment. Howling and yelling and cursing rent the air. The gamblers of Battle Mountain found that these quiet-looking Missouri boys were incarnate devils when roused. But they had most to find out yet. There were four against thirty! Rather heavy odds! The lights were suddenly put out, and Jesse cried:

"Stand aside! Be ready!"

Frank and the other two men knew precisely what that meant. They made a rush for the door amidst shots flying fast and free. Jesse covered their retreat with his pistol. They, having escaped, began to fire warily on the demoralized crowd. Jesse then made for the door, but two burly men, with huge knives, stood in the way. Jesse fired on one of them, and he sank groaning to the earth. In a moment he sprang upon the other and dealt him so powerful a blow with the butt end of his pistol that he fell insensible on his dying comrade. Over this bloody barricade Jesse crept and joined his friends outside.

When lights were obtained the interior of that gambling hell presented a ghastly sight. The half-drunken women were suddenly sobered. Three men lay dead, wallowing in pools of their own blood. Five others lay mortally wounded, groaning, cursing and blaspheming. The floor and walls were all bedabbled with human blood. A sudden impulse stirred a number of the survivors to follow and avenge this dreadful night on the escaped Missourians.

A little more than a mile away they came upon the Jameses and their two friends. The leaders of the avenging mob ran yelling and howling toward them.

"Fall back!" cried Jesse, "fall back! We have fought once in self-defense, and we can fight again." Then, turning to his comrades, he said: "Steady, boys! Let every shot count."

On came the yelling pack, filling the air with blasphemous threatenings of death to the fugitive ones.

"Back, you d——d miscreants! Stand back, I say!" cried Jesse James.

But they rushed forward at the top of their speed.

"Boys, we are in for it," said Jesse, quietly.

"All right! Be ready!" Then he shouted: "Come on, d——n you! Just come ahead and be killed!"

Four bullets, quick and sharp, sped their way to the oncoming mob, and in a moment four men fell wounded to the earth. The Missourians opened fire again, and two others fell gashed and wounded. At this the avengers paused. The dauntless four in that moment escaped. The gamblers, however, treated them to a parting shot, seriously wounding one of the party. Jesse's hat was shot off his head, but no further damage was done. They reached Minnemunca in safety. They had *"shaken up"* Battle Mountain with a vengeance! Twelve men had fallen victims, and were dead or dying! This was a new sensation in the great mining State. The quiet, inoffensive-looking boys, who seemed to have more of the Sunday-school teacher about them than the wild desperado, had left their unmistakable sign manual in the gold-diggers' camp.

It was not safe for our heroes to try the experiment of eating their Christmas dinner in the neighborhood of the Sierras. After that fatal night at Battle Mountain they became marked men. They remained in seclusion only a few days, and then they journeyed with all speed to their home in Missouri.

CHAPTER IV.

ROBBERY OF THE GALLATIN AND COLUMBIA BANKS.

On the 16th of December, 1869, Gallatin, a flour-ishing little city in Daviess county, Missouri, had an experience similar to that of Russelville, the chief difference being that cold-blooded murder was added to that of robbery. It was a dark, gloomy day, such as abound in the month of December. It was supposed that the bank was just then pretty flush in funds. All at once a band of armed horse-men rushed into the quiet street that runs like an ar-tery through Gallatin. With wild cries and curses they ordered all the inhabitants to keep their houses at peril of instant death. Two of the band rushed into the bank (believed to be Cole Younger and Jesse James), and, holding a revolver before the face of Capt. John W. Sheets, demanded that he give up the keys. The safe door was already open. The booty was secured. The amount, however, was small, reaching only about $700. The gold being put in a bag, the robber who had held Captain Sheets in silence deliberately fired a bullet through his brain, and the unfortunate cashier fell dead at his assassin's feet. The robbery completed and the murder done, the wild band fled from Gallatin as quickly as they entered, and left no trace behind them save the plundered bank and the lifeless form of a gallant gentleman who was universally respected. The wanton cruelty of this murder awoke the bitterest feeling throughout the whole neighborhood. Captain Sheets was a great favorite in business and social circles. The robbery was altogether lost sight of in the graver consideration of the foul and unnatural murder, the motive for which it was hard to imagine. It was, however, afterwards averred that the murderer mistook him for a certain Lieutenant Cox, who, it was said, in a raid against the guerrillas had killed the notorious Bill Anderson. The whole country was roused, and a most exciting chase took place. But the robbers were well mounted, and, though they were pursued to the borders of Clay county, the pursuit was in vain, for at that point they lost all track of them.

Governor McClury declared that he did not believe that the James boys had anything to do with

the robbery. For a time his decision had some influence on public opinion, but there was a deep un-
dercurrent of feeling that if these young men, Frank
and Jesse James, had not been actually concerned in
the operations, they were nevertheless parties to, if
not instigators of, the plot. As years went on,
further developments led to the now thoroughly received opinion that Captain Sheets died at the hands
of Frank and Jesse James. Amongst those who believed most thoroughly in the guilt of the James
brothers was Capt. John Thomason, of Clay
county, Missouri. He thought that it was no use in
the world to deal in half measures with these miscreants. He was persuaded that there would be no
peace, no security for life or property, as long as
they were at large, hence he put himself at the head
of a band of men who were resolved at all hazards
and at any cost to arrest Frank and Jesse James and
bring them to justice. Captain Thomason had
served during the war on the Confederate side; he
had also sustained the office of Sheriff of Clay
county to the great admiration of the county at
large. He carried with him great moral influence as
a man who was the outspoken friend of law and order. No man in Clay county could command a

larger following for any good purpose. The James brothers were made acquainted with the purpose of Captain Thomason; they knew the man they had to deal with, but they were not in the least dismayed. They went out to meet him and his band. The meeting is said to have taken place near the home of the Samuels. Captain Thomason demanded their immediate unconditional surrender. Of course, as may be well supposed, they laughed the demand to scorn, and seemed disposed to treat the whole affair as a huge farce. When the thing assumed a more serious aspect and Captain Thomason hinted at force, then there was nothing for it but to meet fire with fire. And the guerrilla boys proved themselves ready for the encounter. A shot from Jesse's pistol brought down Captain Thomason's horse dead under him. The fray lasted only a few minutes. The pursuing party felt that to proceed would only be to endanger life, with little prospect of capturing their prey, so they returned, and Frank and Jesse rode back home scathless and triumphant.

Captain Thomason was annoyed at his defeat, and did not hesitate to express himself in unmeasured terms, not staying even to express very strong and uncompromising opinions concerning Mrs. Samuels,

whom he regarded as the hateful guiding spirit of
these murderous sons. Indeed, he said over and
over again that only such a mother could bring forth
such sons. A remarkable and characteristic inter-
view between the two is reported.

Mrs. Samuels had heard of the strong things Captain Thomason was saying, and thought perhaps to
intimidate him by threats. Whatever was the purpose, this irrepressible woman, now close on sixty
years of age, rode ten miles on horseback to give
Captain Thomason a piece of her mind. She entered
the house without ceremony as the family was din-
ing, and, walking up to Captain Thomason, in a
resolute tone of voice said:

"Captain Thomason, I understand you have called
me a ——!"

"Yes, I did," returned the Captain, "and I want
you to understand that I mean every word I say,
and, mark me, if ever I or any of mine are injured
by you or yours in the least thing, I swear before
heaven and earth that there shall not be a stone left
of your house nor a single member of your family
spared!"

"Indeed!" said the stern-faced woman.

"And if any killing is to be done," continued the

Captain, "take my advice and see you kil' all my family; don't let a member survive, or the injury might be avenged."

At this Mrs. Samuels, with a look of supreme disgust, strode out of the room and journeyed home, feeling that her errand had been a failure.

The spring of 1872 found Frank and Jesse James and the three Younger boys all in Kentucky, whither they generally fled when danger threatened. They had many friends in Kentucky, and were as secure there as any place in the world.

A whole year or more had passed since the last bank raid, and the public mind began to rest in a sense of security. Besides which, the managers of banks, as may well be expected, looked more diligently to the means and methods of security and defense. But while there is no insurmountable difficulty in guarding against ordinary dangers, the special and unexpected and sudden dangers are not so easily foreseen.

Columbia is a pleasant little village in the County of Adair, in Kentucky. A quiet, sleepy little place that knew nothing to disturb the even tenor of its way, save when the holding of the Courts of Session stirred the dull monotony of the place.

On the afternoon of April 29th, 1872, all was in statu quo. It was about 2 o'clock in the afternoon. The bank was still open. The President of the Bank of Deposit was chatting with Mr. R. A. C. Martin, the respected cashier of the bank, and Mr. Garnett, an old citizen of Columbia. All in a moment the conversation was interrupted by a most unusual occurrence. Five well-armed horsemen dashed into the street. There was the old order. Promiscuous firing of pistols, oaths and threatenings; every human being was driven into the house on peril of instant death. Before the gentlemen in the bank could for a moment guess the meaning of this strange tumult, Frank James and Cole Younger dismounted and entered the bank. Without a word the bandits went round the counter, each holding a pair of cocked pistols in his hands.

"Will you give up the safe keys, d——n you?" said one of them to the cashier, holding a pistol within a yard of his head.

"I will not!" was the answer of the brave cashier, Martin.

"Then, d——n you, will you open the same? Come, quick. I've no time to waste. If you don't I'll blow your brains out! Quick, d——n you, quick! Now will you?"

"I will not. I will d——"

Poor, brave Martin had no time to finish the sentence. A bullet crashed through his temples. Blood and brains spurted out upon counter and floor, and the valiant guardian of the public funds fell dead at his murderer's feet.

The onlookers seemed paralyzed. They were horror-stricken and utterly powerless. The robbers then gathered together all they could, which only amounted to a little over $300 in cash. For the robbers had outwitted themselves. The secret of the combination was with the dead cashier. Placing such spoils as they had in hand in a sack, they remounted their horses and gave the signal for departure. They went as quickly as they came.

No sooner had the news of the raid spread than another of those fruitless pursuits began. The robbers were pursued to the mountains of Tennessee. One of the robbers called Saunders, but better known as Bill Longly, the Texan desperado, was shot in Fentress county. The fact that Saunders was of this gang was proof sufficient in the minds of the Kentuckians that the robbers of the Columbia bank were none other than the James and Younger gangs. There are others, however, who cling to the belief that neither Frank nor Jesse had any part in this fray.

Russelville! Gallatin! Columbia!

CHAPTER V.

ROBBERY OF THE CORYDON (IOWA) BANK.

In less than twelve months after the robberies nar-
rated in the preceding chapter the Bank of Corydon,
Iowa, was in like manner robbed and raided. It was
on the 28th of June, 1873, at about 10 o'clock in the
morning. The bank was just opening for business,
when seven desperadoes charged furiously into the
center of the town, firing right and left and swearing
to shoot dead everybody who remained in the streets.
Their commands were obeyed. The streets were
cleared. None of the inhabitants thought of offering
any resistance. Three of the robbers dismounted and,
with cocked pistols, entered the bank, swearing to blow
the heads off any who dared to interfere with them.
The six heavy dragoon pistols served to terrify those
who were in the bank, and, with the memories of Captain Sheets and Mr. Martin before them, they yielded
at discretion. The safe was opened and the contents
thrown into a sack. It is said that the robbers made

by this one haul a sum nearly approaching $40,000. The people in the bank were charged to order and silence, and one of the robbers' brood boasted that he could fetch a button off the coat of any of them with his pistol; so they had best have a care.

Of course, after the consternation had given place to quieter moments, the inhabitants instituted a vigorous pursuit. The common result followed. Not one of the robbers were caught.

A most amusing story is told of Jesse, who on this memorable occasion played the part of rustic to his heart's content. It was the second day after the bank robbery at Corydon, Iowa. The whole region was up in arms and in hot pursuit after the robbers. Jesse was riding along a road not much frequented, when he became suddenly aware of two men riding in hot fury not far distant. Confident that they had neither seen nor heard him, his ready wit suggested a speedy course of action. Jesse was dressed in the rough attire of a granger, and assumed a most uncouth simplicity of dialect and manners. When he came within reasonable distance of the two well-armed, well-mounted horsemen, he, with a wary eye on their pistols and his hand not far from his own, accosted them:

"Well, gentlemen, hev you met anybody up the road

ridin' a hoss an leadin' on another one, 'cause you see as how I lives down on the Nodaway, an' some infernal theif has gone off with my two best hosses. I hearn about two miles furder down, at the blacksmith shop, that a man passed there about a hour an' a half ago with two hosses, an' they fits the descripshun of mine to a T. Have you seen sich?"

"No. Where are you traveling from?"

"Why, Lord, I've come all the way from the Nordaway. The infernal thieves are using us up awful. I wish I'd come on the infernal son of a seacock who's taken my hosses, I do. You bet, I'd go for him with these 'ere irons. I would that!" And Jesse revealed his "weapons," as he called them.

"Did you see anybody on the road ahead?" asked the tallest of the two horsemen.

"Not for some miles. I met four ugly-looking customers this mornin'. They looked like they might 'a been hoss thieves. D——n the hoss thieves, say I," said the rustic Jesse.

"Thieves are plenty now-a-days. They come into towns and break banks in open daylight. How far did you say the four men were ahead?"

"Well, I didn't say, but it must be more'n two hours since I met 'em, an' they were a ridin' purty fast, an'

I've rid my hoss almost down, as you can see," answered Jesse.

"What kind of looking men were they?" asked the robber-hunters.

"Well, one was a sizeable man, with a long, red beard and a flopped black hat on, a ridin' on a chestnut hoss, an' one more was a smallish man, with very black hair and beard, and sharp black eyes, an' he was a ridin' on a roan hoss, an' another was an oldish man, with some gray among his beard, an' he wore a blue huntin' shirt coat, an' he was a ridin' a gray hoss, and the last feller was a little weazle-faced chap, with tallowy complexion, who didn't wear no beard, an' he rode on a dark-brown hoss," said the rustic, with rustic simplicity.

The two robber-hunters then consulted together.

"That's their description," said one. "Precisely," said the other. "Shall we follow?" asked one. "I would like to," replied the other. "But there are four of them," was the remark in rejoinder. "Yes, that is bad. If Ed, Dick and Will would just hurry up. Those fellows are no doubt very dangerous men," was the comment of one. "You bet they are," was the response.

All this time Jesse had listened as an interested

party. Now he thought he was privileged to make an inquiry.

"What's up, strangers, anyhow?" Jesse asked.

"You blow it! Don't you know that the Corydon Bank, up in Iowa, was robbed yesterday?"

Jesse opened his eyes in well-feigned surprise.

"You don't say so!" he ejaculated.

"Yes, in broad daylight, and the men you met are the robbers, no doubt. There's a big reward offered to catch them."

"What's this country comin' to, anyhow? Hoss-thieves down on the Nodaway an' bank rogues up to Iowa. 'Pears like hard-workin', honest folks can't get along much more," grumbled Jesse.

"Could you go back with us?"

"I'd like to, but the cussed hoss-thieves will get away. Besides, you see my hoss is mighty nigh played out hisself. Howsumever, I might ride with you as fur as I can. D——n all thieves, say I; don't you?"

And Jesse actually turned round with the two pursuers of the robbers in pursuit of another posse of pursuers which Jesse had been enabled accurately to describe by having seen them pass while lying snug in a dense thicket.

"They might catch the robbers, an' as he'd have a

sheer ov the reward, it would be better'n nothing at all fur his stolin hosses."

For miles Jesse rode with them, till, coming near a railway station, he begged to be excused on the ground that his horse was becoming lame. His excuse was accepted, and he left the pursuers to their vain and hopeless pursuit.

CHAPTER VI.

CHICAGO, ROCK ISLAND AND PACIFIC TRAIN ROBBERY.

During the spring of the year in the early seventies Frank James and Jim Younger were sent into Nebraska to gather all the information they could relative to the express service, and especially the shipment of bullion and precious treasure from the West.

The remaining company began to feel impatient of the long delay of their comrades, so to break up the monotony and replenish the failing coffers of the gang, Jesse James, Bill Chadwell, Clell Miller and Bob and Cole Younger resolved on one more bank robbery. The Savings Association Bank of Ste. Genevieve was fixed upon as the scene of their lawless endeavors.

Ste. Genevieve is a grand old Catholic town of Missouri. It is more than a century old—the home and scene of French Catholic taste and politeness. The dwellers in this Missouri paradise were a wise, thrifty people, and their savings bank was known to contain often as much as $100,000—the accumulated savings of a well-to-do, thrifty commuity.

It was a beautiful spring morning, the 27th of May, 1873. Ste. Genevieve was looking its very loveliest. Mr. O. D. Harris, the cashier of the bank, accompanied by F. A. Rozier, a son of the Hon. Forman A. Rozier, the president of the bank, had left his garden home all bright and cheerful, little dreaming what an episode was at hand. The cashier and his young companion arrived at the bank, the door swung open, and suddenly Mr. Harris and young Rozier were confronted by four armed men and accosted thus:

"We have come to help you to open the bank. Open the safe instantly, d——n you; we have no time to lose."

"I am helpless and cannot resist you," replied the overpowered Mr. Harris.

Meantime another of the robbers pointed a pistol at the head of young Rozier, and called out:

"You keep still, d——d little rat, if you don't want to have your brains blown out in an instant!"

"I? What for?" asked the young clerk, who had shown signs of desiring to create an alarm.

"Not another word, young devil," said his stern-faced foe; "that's enough! A blabbing tongue c... be stopped d——d easy."

Taking advantage of the moment, and desiring that these strange visitors should have all his room and none of his company, he made a bold leap and sprang down the steps of the bank into the street. As he fled the fellow fired at him and cried: "Halt! halt! you wretched young cuss!"

The bullet tore through the shoulder of his coat and grazed his chin.

The report of a bullet roused the attention of a gentleman opposite, who seized his gun and was about to join the fray in defense of Mr. Harris, but the good man's wife exhorted her spouse to mind his own business. Like a wise man, he obeyed, and doing so probably saved his own life and that of Mr. Harris.

By this time the safe was opened. But the robbers were much disappointed, for instead of making a haul of something like $80,000 or $100,000, they only secured booty to the extent of about $8,500. Mr. Harris was then relieved of a beautiful gold watch which he wore, and the robbers then started away.

Just as they were leaving the city one of the horses of the robbers ran away, and the bag containing their ill-gotten gains broke in the street. It was but the work of a moment to lay violent hands on a German farmer who had a wagon and team. They made him, under threat of instant death, ride after the runaway horse, the rest of them guarding the treasure till his return. The citizens were up to the condition of things and began to arm and prepare for a battle. But the German farmer returned with the runaway horse, and the robbers mounted and rode off. A dozen men were by this time ready for pursuit, and they gave chase and came very near to the runaways. The company of plunderers turned, and, facing their pursuers, swore by everything that was terrible that if they came one step nearer they would shoot them dead. The wise and heroic twelve at once returned.

The results of the pioneer journey of Frank James and Bill Younger into Nebraska were now under consideration. The method of bank raiding was growing quite monotonous. They longed for some novelty to be imported into their robber experience. Early in the month of July—the Jameses and the Youngers and Robert Moore—a new importation—a desperado from the Indian Territory, held a council of war in Jackson county, Missouri.

The subject for consideration was to find the best and most successful method of robbing a railway train.

The first scheme, to rob a train on the Hannibal and St. Joe Railway, was rejected. The pros and cons were fully gone into, and it was at last determined to make Iowa the scene of this first train-wrecking experiment. Comanche Tony—a desperate Texan ranger—was added to the plundering brotherhood. The gang, comprising the James boys, the Youngers, Bob Moore, and this Texan Tony, met—each, of course, coming different ways—at a point about fourteen miles east of the city of Council Bluffs, on the Chicago, Rock Island and Pacific Railway.

The train was due to pass their point of ambush about three o'clock in the morning. All night they waited and watched, scarcely exchanging a word with each other, and when they did, not above a whisper. Three or four rails were loosened and torn from their places. Several cross-ties were placed in position to be used the moment they were required. They worked and watched and waited in silence. They had chosen a most suitable spot. It was fourteen miles from Council Bluffs, six miles from Adair, and about the same distance from Des Moines. There was not a single human habitation for miles around.

The rumbling of the train was heard in the distance. The gang set to work with awful dogged determination. As the train crossed the Turkey Creek bridge the loosened rails were thrown apart and half a dozen cross-ties were thrown across the track just above.

The glaring headlight showed to the vigilant eye of John Rafferty, the trusty engineer of the train, the danger ahead.

But he saw too late!

The train was speeding to its doom at the rate of twenty-five miles an hour!

"My God, the rails move!" yelled John Rafferty to his fireman.

With this wild cry on his lips, and a wilder look in his eye, the brave engineer reversed the engine and applied the air brakes. But it was in vain! The gigantic wheels sped over the sixty feet of firm iron that lay before them, the engine, like a wild demon goaded on to madness, ploughed into the bank and rolled over on its side.

The air-brakes had stopped the train, but the concussion had killed the valiant Rafferty, who lay with upturned face dead on that bright summer Sunday morning! Dead because he did his duty!

Then followed a scene of indescribable confusion and horror! Amid the screams and cries of half-

awakened women and children the robbers set to work,
yelling—not like Indians in honorable warfare—but
rather like demons set on fire with the madness of hell,
these desperadoes rushed forth, discharging their pistols through the coach windows, demanding in the
most lordly style that every passenger should keep
still. They then rushed into the cars, firing over the
heads of the inmates, to alarm and terrify them. If
any man ventured to go forward or leave his seat
under any pretense, a revolver was held before his
face and a threat, supported by an awful oath, that if
he dared to wink an eyelid, he should die the death of
a dog.

The express car was broken into and the messenger
in charge had his arm broken and was forced to un-
lock the safe. The robbers secured some $6,000, and
the poor guardian of the mails had his watch taken
and ten dollars, the only money he possessed. After
this every passenger was searched and robbed of
money and jewelry. The spoils were put in a sack
and the masked robbers sought their horses, and as the
light broadened that peaceful summer morning they
took their way southward, $25,000 richer for their
dreadful exploit.

A reward of $50,000 was offered for their arrest.
But it was offered in vain.

CHAPTER VII

FIGHT AT THE MEXICAN FANDANGO.

! Shortly after the Chicago, Rock Island and Pacific robbery Frank and Jesse James made their way into Texas, and one day they rode well mounted into Matamoras. It was a gay season. What season is not gay to the light hearts of Mexicans? A fandango, a sort of ball on a small scale, was announced, and Frank and Jesse, nothing loth, resolved to see what was to be seen and have their share of the fun. The night came, and the hall was well filled with olive-eyed, swarthy senoritas and gay-looking hidalgoes.

The band struck up, and the fair Mexican damsels began to dance. Their graceful movements soon stirred the pulses of the robber brothers. They joined the festive dance. They were not celebrated as graceful dancers, and the intricate gyrations of the mazy Spanish dance was quite too much for them. No doubt they were clumsy, and their awkwardness would be all the more manifest when contrasted by the ex-

quisite grace of every movement of their partners.
The on-lookers were first amused and then broke out
into open ridicule, and laughed at Frank and Jesse
and began to mimic, with exaggerated contortions, the
awkward dancing of the brothers.

Now, the boys could stand a good deal, but you
were not to laugh at them. They were not very fas-
tidious or exacting in their demands, but they would
not stand being laughed at! So, quick as thought
down went one of the boldest beneath the strong hand
of Frank. In a moment a strongly-built Mexican
struck Frank a blow on the cheek which sent him
spinning headlong into the ample laps of two Mexican maidens, much to their astonishment and disgust.
This was no time to waver, so Jesse improved the moment by sending a bullet through the brain of the
Mexican who had struck his brother Frank. This
stirred the Spanish blood, and, what lovers of the san-
guinary would say, the fun began, and the fighting
was beautiful. Frank and Jesse made for the door,
but their way was blocked by the furious and vengeful
hidalgoes. Stilettos gleamed and glittered. Frank and
Jesse both struck and stabbed. But stilettos are poor
where revolvers come. These Mexicans kept the
doorway for a time, but after the boys had used their

pistols a few times four Mexicans lay dead on the threshold, and six others were dreadfully wounded.

The Mexicans had blockaded that door, but the boys' of Missouri raised the blockade! Just at the passage from the hall a vengeful Spaniard was aiming a deadly blow at Frank's heart, but Jesse intervened and lodged a bullet in the would-be murderer's heart. He fell and stuck the dagger in the floor as he fell. Escaping from the room, they made for their horses. Jesse ran first, but Frank was pursued by three of these hidalgoes. Frank had seized a bludgeon on his way, and now, turning at bay, faced his followers, and with almost Herculean strength he laid the three Mexicans stunned and motionless at his feet. The boys got on their horses and rode away; but they were pursued, and there was nothing for it but to make a bold plunge for the Rio Grande, which they did, and swam safely to the further shore.

They had paid a dollar at eight o'clock for a night's fun at the fandango. Jesse said, his face rippling with humor, spite of the pain of several stiletto wounds:

"Well, Frank, old boy, guess we got our dollar's worth of exciting amusement out of that gang!"

"You bet!" was Frank's laconic reply. The boys had to go into quarantine at a little town called Concapcion. Here they remained under surgical care for three months, so perverse were the wounds they had received in the fandango at Matamoras, on the banks of the Rio Grande.

Carmen, a town in the northern part of the State of Chihauhua, Mexico, next saw the two James brothers. This town was on the highway of travel for Mexican merchants and silver coming from the mines.

One fair May morning six pack mules, each guided by a separate muleteer, and each mule bearing the glittering burden of 150 pounds of solid silver on his back, moved out of the city of Chihuahua. Beside these there were twelve men as a guard. In all, eighteen men to guard the precious treasure. All went well till they reached Carmen, and then two simple-minded, guileless-looking young Americans entered into general conversation with the guards, and by the Socratic method of gentle inquiry possessed themselves of the knowledge necessary to help them in due time to possess the silver. No Scotchman ever felt more attached to his "siller" than did these American young gentlemen at Carmen. Then our boys—for, of course, the reader understands that these quiet young men were Frank and Jesse James—assumed to make confidantes of these Mexican guards. They wanted to

get back to the United States, but they had heard so
much of the peril of the way that they were quite
timid at taking the journey. What with Indians and
guerrillas they were quite afraid to venture. Frank
and Jesse had three other friends who were really in
the same box with themselves. The chief of the
guard was interviewed with a request that he would
allow these young men, who had been inspecting
mines, to go under their escort for safety just across
the perilous border, of course, agreeing that if danger
came they would fight in the interests of the guard
and their treasure.

The chief consented, and so there started out next
day from Carmen the procession of mules and their
treasures and guards, and these five pious-looking
young gentlemen — goody-goody-looking enough to
teach in Sunday school or exhort at a mission. And
yet Mexico had not five such desparadoes from the
North Fork to the most southerly sweep of the Rio
Grande!

For two or three days they were watched, but soon
all suspicion gave way to confidence. It was noon,
about the fifth day out, the cavalcade halted near a
most refreshing fountain. The burdens were taken
from the mules that they might graze at leisure in the

valley. The muleteers and guards, all save two—who were reserved to stand sentinel over the bags of silver—were enjoying their noonday siesta. The ingenious five were under a tree apart, holding a quiet converse. The whole guns of the party were stacked against a tree. The two guards on duty over the silver pouches were holding their guns in the most formal and careless manner over their shoulders.

The opportune moment had come!

"Let's go, boys!" was the brief signal from Jesse, accompanied by his low, shrill whistle.

Crack! went a couple of pistols, and the two armed guards sank quivering to the earth, shot dead! The arms stacked against the tree were destroyed in less time than it takes to tell. The other guards were ordered to hold up their arms, and were at once disarmed. They then ordered the muleteers to put the bags of silver on the best mules. All the rest of the horses were shot. Then Frank and Jesse and their confreres rode off with their stolen treasure, threatening instant death to any one who dared to follow. The robbers bore their treasure into Texas, divided the spoils, and congratulated each other on the success of their enterprise.

Nine hundred pounds of silver, to be divided among

five robbers! Not an ounce of the silver was ever traced to the robbers, nor were one of them ever brought to justice. The Mexican merchants would henceforth be most careful how they undertook the guardianship of innocent-looking young American gentlemen.

There is a spot on the River of the North called Piedras Negras, which is known as the meeting place of all sorts of strange characters—brigands from the passes of the Sierras Madres; thieves from Mata-moras; cut-throats from Saltilio; smugglers from all the border line. And now to this appropriate region come the James brothers in the spring of 1877. They both of them anticipated there would be, to use their own phrase, "plenty of fun," and in this sup-position they were not destined to be mistaken. They soon got all the fun they wanted.

Riding leisurely together one day through one of the villages not far from Piedras Negras, they were observed by a number of Mexican raiders, who prob-ably thought there was the chance for a good haul, and accordingly the enterprising Mexicans proposed to try their luck. The boys quickened their pace after they left the village, and soon found they were pursued by a dozen or more half drunken, howling

Mexicans, who fired off pistols madly and wildly, as though to impress the young men who had ridden through their village what kind of daredevils they had to deal with. To the utter dismay of this roystering troop, our boys, instead of flying in hot haste before them, deliberately turned round and faced their pursuers, and in a brief space four of the foremost of the rabble squad lay sprawling on the ground, with their right arms broken from the bullets of Frank's and Jesse's pistols. They at once retreated to the village in hot haste, and Frank and Jesse, as if mad for mischief and heedless of peril, returned also. A regular fusillade ensued. Bullets rained upon them to their heart's content; they left two greasers dead upon the plaza as relics of their visit, and then passed on. That night, as they crossed a stream swollen by the rains of spring, they were surprised by ten brigands in ambush on the opposite side of the bank. Fire was opened, and Jesse received a small wound in the left shoulder. This incited their anger, and the brothers charged into their hiding place, and everyone fled, save one who lay stark and dead that night, a victim to his own folly and the sure aim of Frank James.

In the course of their wonderings they came to

Monclova, a large town in Coahuila, and here, to their surprise, they met one of their old companions of the guerrilla days. He had returned after Quantrell's death to peaceful pursuits, and having become enamored of the bright, piercing eyes of a Mexican girl, he had married and settled down to a quiet, happy life. But the sight of the James boys and the sound of their voices woke up a thousand pleasant memories. They talked of the old times, and sang the old songs, and fought the old battles over again, till the Mexican bride was alarmed to think how desperate a man she had married.

Now, it seems the one essential proof of Mexican kindness is to honor your friend who visits you with a fandango. Frank and Jesse, nothing loth, on the promise that the grace and beauty of Monclova should adorn the scene, accepted the honor. The night came, and with the night the fandango.

The honored guests were summering in beauty's smiles, the host was charmed that all went so well, and the gentle hostess beamed and smiled complacently around. All went well for a time, till the quick eye of Jesse thought he discovered a furtive glance in the eyes of two of the guests. A young lieutenant of the Mexican army and an American

gentleman from Matehuala were among the guests.
They were conversing in low tones, and looked, as
Jesse thought, strangely at Frank and himself.
Frank was making love to a fair senorita when Jesse
called his attention to these signs of mischief. But
Frank thought Jesse was making the best use of
his imagination. Jesse began to think he had seen
both these men before, and when, after a little while,
this mysterious pair departed, he became more and
more convinced that danger was brewing. And
forewarned, forearmed, he advised Frank to be on
th alert. He was not mistaken; these gentlemen
both knew Frank and Jesse. Both men owed the
boys a grudge, for one had lost a brother at their
hands in 1865, and the other a friend not more than
a year ago. Again, there was still an offer of $50,000
for their heads from the American authorities. Captain Macy still held Governor Pillsbury's offer good
of $1,000 each for the capture of the bandits. There
was money to be made, and fame and honor. So the
authorities were at once addressed, and in the dead
of the night a muster was ordered and a detachment
of some eighty was at once brought to the fandango.
The place was thoroughly surrounded. When the
festivities were at tneir gayest the doors were un-

ceremoniously thrown open and a stately officer strode into the room, followed by a military guard.

A scene of indescribable confusion ensued. The men were astounded, the ladies were panic-stricken. The only calm people at the fandango were the two most concerned.

The officer marched up to Frank and Jesse, and in the name of the Mexican Government demanded their surrender. The brothers laughed derisively in the faces of the officers.

"Will you surrender peacefully?" he asked.

"Never!" was Frank's calm reply.

With that the officer motioned to his guards to move up.

"Stop!" It was Jesse's voice of command. The officer waved the guards to halt.

"We have a proposition to submit. Will you hear it?"

"If it means surrender, yes," replied the officer.

"It is this," pursued Jesse, not appearing to notice the purport of the officer's reply, "allow these ladies here to retire, and we will discuss the question with you."

"I shall be compelled to take you by force," said the officer.

' Let the ladies retire," I say!" exclaimed Jesse James, in a tone that betrayed his impatience."

The officer intimated that opposition was really useless. The house was surrounded. Yet he mortally hated to begin an affray in the presence of the ladies, who were excited enough already, and probably, if matters had gone to immediate issue, would have flung themselves, a fair bulwark of defense, before the young American gentlemen, who had been so "awfully nice" all the evening, and who were now being so shamefully ill-used.

"Let the ladies retire;" repeated Jesse, as though he were commanding officer.

The ballroom was soon cleared of the fair ones.

"Now," said the officer, "lay down your pistols. I have an ample guard to enforce these orders. The house is surrounded. You cannot get away."

Before the sentence was well out of his mouth the officer lay dead at Jesse's feet, with a bullet lodged in his proud heart.

Quick as thought the guard started forward, unable to realize that their leader was dead.

One, two, three! Sharp, short and quick! A deafening report, three whiffs of smoke, and three soldiers lying in pools of blood that flow from the fountains of their own hearts.

It was an awful sight! Were these men demons instead of men? All the evening they had been polite and gentle and bland; and now in two minutes four men lay dead at their feet, and they looked as if every man who thwarted them must suffer a like fate.

The guard became demoralized and fled. The boys now rushed for the street. The soldiers guarding the house fired, but they fired aimlessly in their wild confusion, and Frank and Jesse only received a few scratches.

In a little while the whole town was mad with excitement, and the wildest stories got abroad. All the ladies of the fandango had been remorselessly butchered by hireling murderers, the soldiers were all shot, and the work of massacre was going on. The wild stories grew and grew. The streets soon surged with a most excited crowd. The fire bells rang, the alarm drums beat at the barracks, the whole of the soldiery formed in line and marched to the scene of the disaster. Men, women and children made the night hideous with their screams. The darkness was dense and favored the fugitives. Frank and Jesse reached their horses, and while Monclova was hunting them about the region of the place of blood they were

"Over the hills and far away!"

And for sometime Frank and Jesse kept their abode in the mountains, and it was not till all was over and almost forgotten that they ventured to turn their faces from the scene of blood. Not that for one moment they held themselves culpable of any wrong. It was defensive warfare, and all is fair in love and war.

And so Frank and Jesse dug four graves in Monclova, though it must be admitted they did not invite the fray.

Juan Fernando Palacio had won the fame of being the most bloodthirsty and relentless of all that vile robber brood that infested the Piedras Negras, Eagle Pass and Meir, on the Upper Rio Grande. The James brothers were now to test their prowess alongside this notorious freebooter and his bloody-minded followers. He was the captain and guide of thirty daring, unscrupulous men. The Valley of the Pecos, where Frank and Jesse were now residing, was rich in flocks and herds, and it was the sole ambition of Palacio to sweep these herds from the peaceful vale and utterly discomfit the "cow boys," as he and his followers disdainfully called the dwellers in the Pecos.

The time for the stampede was fixed, and, assisted
by a murderer who rejoiced in the name of Jesus Almonte, an outlaw from all civilized society, Palacio
proposed to carry away all the cattle, and if the cow-
boys on the various ranches objected—well, cold
lead and a short shrift. And the cold lead first. The
stampede was complete. Three of the "cow boys"
were killed, but the herds were marched to the banks
of the Rio Grande. Two days afterwards Frank
and Jesse heard of this from one of the sorely dis-
tressed herdsmen. It so happened that Frank and
Jesse had possessions in the valley, and their flocks
had been carried off by the murdering Mexicans;
and of all men they were not the men to sit down
and be robbed in silence. Their plans were soon
formed. Prompt action was needed now. It was in
October. Frank and Jesse soon got on Palacio's
trail. They came to El Paso. All was silent, though
the robbers had driven through the village. Palacio
and Almonte came to camp in the mountains. They
felt themselves quite secure, and so fell asleep in
fancied safety. But they had but little sleeping time.
They were suddenly aroused by reports from the
avenging pistols of the James boys. Shot after shot
was fired, dealing death at every discharge. Roused

from the midst of a fitful sleep, the robbers were dazed and bewildered, and thought they were surrounded by a huge company of avengers, and so they fled as fast as their weary legs could carry them, giving themselves no time, for they were in no mood to examine the state of things. Ten of these robbers lay dead, and the rest, terror-stricken, had hurried away in wild confusion to the shelter of the hills. The leaders, Palacio and Almonte, were not with the camp when Frank and Jesse made their murderous onslaught. When the tidings reached them they, of course, imagined what the rest of the thirty thought— that there must be a company of avengers, or "Grino Diablas," as they called them, from the Pecos Vale. When they came to understand that this successful raid had been carried on by two men only, they were furious, and swore by all their gods to be avenged. The whole troop of the twenty-five were on the trail of the brothers to recapture the cattle and strike death to the hearts of the graceless two who had wrought them such humiliation and decimated their band.

At last they came in sight of the great crowding herds of cattle, and there were only these two men to deal with. Who would now give a pin's worth for the chances of the boys? And yet we have seen how, again and again, when their peril was the direst, they were the calmest; and so often have they rode straight up to the very jaws of death and returned scathless, that they at least must not be buried even in our thought till they are quite dead. The boys had one advantage—they carried with them long-range, sixteen-shot Winchester rifles. Five of the Mexicans, dead shots all of them, were detailed to finish these "impudent American devils!"

The boys had fastened themselves to their saddles, held their reins between their teeth, and dashed out to meet the furious fire. Their long-range rifles saved them; each picked his man, and in a moment two saddles were empty and two Mexicans fell dead. The astonished three turned to flee away! But it was too late! Two more fell victims to the long range, and only one was left to go back and tell the story of their defeat.

So far they had been remarkably successful. But an imperfect success is worse sometimes than direct defeat. There must be twenty of that band not far away, and Jesse did not feel that the shouting time had come. They were still in the wood, so he quietly observed to Frank:

"I'll ride to that swell over on the left to see what those other devils are doing."

Arrived on the crest of the hill, he saw fifteen of these greasers coming up the hill. They were four hundred yards away, but Jesse's trusted long-range Winchester did splendid service. One after another the Mexicans fell, till by the time Frank came up four of the leaders and one of their mustangs lay dead, and the rest of the company had beat a retreat. As Frank reached the brow of the hill, Jesse said:

"Well, I've prepared a feast for the vultures over yonder."

"How many are down?" asked Frank.

"Oh, only four men and one horse," he answered, with a grim sort of a smile.

And the rest of the valiant Mexican host were galloping away for dear life.

On one occasion, after a prolonged absence, Frank and Jesse found on their return home that a brood of Mexican cattle robbers, under the lead of the infamous Bustenado, had crossed the Rio Grande and made a night raid among the herdsmen. The raid had been swift and well managed, and Bustenado and his tribe were fast making for the other side of the river.

A special element in this raid, that made it doubly astrocious, and just such a raid as the James would feel they were called of Heaven to avenge, was the fact that the bold robbers had carried away their **fair** Alice Gordon, the pride and beauty of the vale.

Gordon, the father of the captured girl, was a Scotchman over seventy years of age, who had been overwhelmed by misfortune in the East, had become misanthropic, and who had sought relief from his troubles in the comparative solitude of the great plains, where there was almost no society and where nature alone could charm him to something of contentment. His daughter Alice, a beautiful young lady of many accomplishments and of strong will, accompanied him. To the few rude men who sometimes sought the hospitality of Gordon, she was the embodiment of all the grace and beauty their imagination could picture, and there was none who would not ride and fight in her behalf without an instant's delay.

There was one and only one redeeming feature in this case. The robbers had not borne her captive alone, for they had taken also a most devoted and attached negro servant, Joe. Joe worshipped the beautiful Alice, and would readily have died for her. Little harm would come to Alice while Joe was near at hand. What their ultimate purpose was in capturing Alice it was hard to tell. She was captured and borne away from her home. That was the first practical fact. The next was, that she was to be rescued, and Frank and Jesse leapt to that task of rescue as gallantly as the knights of old entered the lists for the ladies they loved.

On the morning of the third day's march Frank and Jesse came upon the objects of their search. They determined on an immediate attack. No waiting for the night. No waiting a moment longer than to take in the whole situation, and act with caution as well as promptitude. They were so to act as not to endanger the life of Alice, and yet to bring swift vengeance to the mean and dastardly Bustenado.

The robbers were eating breakfast when first the boys espied them. They were evidently enjoying themselves, laughing merrily over their exploits. The cattle were slaking their thirst at a neighboring spring. At a little distance from the rest Alice Gordon, wearied, sad and heart-broken, was sitting apart, her faithful attendant, the sable Joe, vainly imploring her to eat. The company of the Mexicans was composed of thirty well-practiced robbers. The James boys only mustered six to follow their lead, but what had they not done with as small a number in the years that were gone? The command was given into the hands of Jesse. The little company of avengers had approached within sight. They were ready with their reins between their teeth, a loaded Colt's revolver in each hand. They only waited the word of command. At last it came. A wild yell from Jesse, and the eight sprang upon the unprepared greasers, and before the first awful fire of Jesse and his clan half the Mexicans were killed. The rest, horrified, fled to regain their horses and decamp. The miserable Bustenado led the retreat, and as he gained his horse, with mean and dastard spirit he fired a parting shot aimed at Alice Gordon, who had fainted. His aim happily missed its mark. But Jesse, quick as thought, sent a bullet between his shoulders, and he fell upon his horse's neck, as dead as a bag of sand. Not more than six of the company escaped, and they had the sad work to tell how the weird Americans had strewn the banks of the Rio Grande with the forms of some of the bravest sons of Mexico.

The cattle were turned homeward, and the rescued Alice Gordon sat upon her horse as gay as a queen, and headed the procession back to the Vale of Pecos, where Frank and Jesse James are thought of to this day as brave, heroic men.

CHAPTER VIII.

ROBBERY OF THE MALVERN AND HOT SPRINGS STAGE
AND THE ST. LOUIS AND TEXAS EXPRESS
AT GADSHILL.

On the day of the first stage robbery perpetrated by the James gang the regular stage running from Malvern, on the St. Louis, Iron Mountain and Southern Railway, to Hot Springs had two ambulances for the sick invalids who were seeking such relief from their sufferings as the Hot Springs could afford. It was, however, the resort of the wealthy, not of the poor.

The robbers took advantage of these facts. And as the cavalcade proceeded quietly on its way it came to a most picturesque little spot called Sulphur Vale, near the old Gaines mansion, and about five miles from Hot Springs. The stage stayed for a few moments in order that the horses might quench their thirst from the waters of the Sulphur, after which the whole company proceeded on their journey. They had not gone more than a mile from the watering place when the driver of the stage was suddenly accosted:

"Stop! stop! or I'll blew your head off!"

With this unceremonious challenge, five men, dressed in Federal uniform, sprang from their ambush, each with cocked revolvers in their hands, threatening the lives of every passenger who dared to resist them. Of course, the passengers were struck dumb with consternation and terror. Presence of mind is an uncommonly good thing, but by no means common under such circumstances.

"Come, d——n you! Tumble out quick; we have no time to spare!" was the order of the foremost robber.

"Oh, certainly!" said a Mr. Charles Morse. "We can do nothing else."

"I am paralyzed in my legs and cannot walk," cried a poor old victim of rheumatism within the stage, as the other passengers came tumbling out.

"Never mind! Stay where you are," was the reply.

The stage was emptied, save of the one lame old gentleman. The rest of the passengers were ordered, with oaths and threats, and with pointed revolvers to confirm the threats, to form in a circle and hold up their hands, which they did without delay.

"Stop! stop! or I'll blow your head off!"

The brigands then began to search, examine and rob every passenger. Not one escaped, and not one seemed equal to offering the least resistance or making the slightest remonstrance. The net result in money and valuables approximated the sum of $4,000. The following may serve to show in detail the strangest bill of merchandise ever made out:

THE SPOILS OF ONE MORNING'S ROBBERY.

Ex-Gov. Burbank, Dakota, cash..........	$850 00
" " " diamond pin...	350 00
" " " gold watch....	250 00
Passenger from Syracuse, N. Y...........	160 00
John Dietrich, Esq., Little Rock, Ark......	200 00
William Taylor, Esq., Lowell, Mass........	650 00
Charles Moore, Esq.....................	70 00
E. A. Peebles, Hot Springs..............	20 00
Three country farmers.................	45 00
Southern Express Company..............	450 00
Geo. R. Crump, Memphis, Tenn..........	45 00
Total..............................$3,090 00

"Not a bad morning's work," says one who counts only the gains of the robbers. But might not these men have earned more by honorable toil than by this sad course of life?

"Within a month, a little month," or ere the memory of the Gains' Place stage robbery had subsided, the robbers were at their tasks again.

This time a train was to be wrecked and robbed. The train selected was the St. Louis and Texas Express, and the place for the exploit was a little lonely flag station on the Iron Mountain Road about a hundred miles south of St. Louis, and about seven miles from Piedmont, just where Shepard Mountain and the Pilot Knob stand lofty guardians of the lonely vale of Arcadia.

It was in the very depth of winter, January 31st, 1874. The cold, biting wintry day was closing. About half-past three o'clock in the afternoon a company of seven men, splendidly mounted and well armed, came to the lonely flag station of Gadshill. The only inhabitants of that bleak region were a station agent, a blacksmith and two or three countrymen. It did not take long to place this small community under arrest, and by the usual threats of violence to ensure their silence. The train was to be boarded in this quiet, uninhabited spot, where it was utterly impossible to give anything like an effective alarm. With the tools from the blacksmith's shop they securely imprisoned their captives, and then set to work to prepare for the coming train.

The signal flag was displayed and the switch opened, so that the train would be inevitably ditched if it attempted to pass. Everything being in order, the robbers waited for their unsuspecting prey.

The train left the Plum Street Depot, St. Louis, about 9.30 o'clock in the morning and was not due till 5.40 o'clock in the evening. The train was in charge of Mr. C. A. Alford, and was well loaded with passengers and express freight. True to time, the train came bowling along, and the engineer, seeing the danger signal ahead, brought the train to a standstill at the little station. No one was seen on the platform. But in a moment Cole Younger mounted the cab of the engine, and at the point of the pistol drew off the engineer and fireman in terror of their lives.

Mr. Alford, the conductor, immediately left the train to see what passengers were waiting to board her, when he was met with this gentle demand:

"Give up your money and your watch, d——n your soul, and quick!"

Mr. Alford gave up about $50 he had in his possession and an elegant gold watch. And then he was hustled most unceremoniously into the little station house that had become a prison.

"Get in there and be quiet, d——n you," was all the brief instruction of the moment.

The train was now wholly in the hands of the robbers. And most effectively they managed their work. Terrifying the passengers by threats and pistols, they induced them with very little hesitation to give up all the valuables they possessed.

One peculiar feature of this raid was that the robbers insisted on knowing the names of their victims. The timid pilgrims readily gave their names. But one, bolder than the rest, was curious to know why the name was demanded.

"What is your name?" asked one of the brigands of a Mr. Newell, who was on the train.

"What do you want to know that for?"

"D——n you, out with your name, and ask questions afterwards!" was the profane reply he received.

"Well, my name is Newell, and here is my money, and now I want to know why you ask for my name?" said Mr. Newell with an attempt at pleasantry, fortified by a sort of grim smile.

"You seem to be a sort of jolly coon, anyhow," said the robber, "and I'll gratify you. That old scoundrel,

Pinkerton, is on his train, or was to have been on it, and we want to get him, so that we can cut out his heart and roast it."

The boys had a mortal hatred of Pinkerton and all the detective clan, much as they despised them. And no doubt if Mr. Allan Pinkerton had been on board and had revealed himself there would have been a somewhat tough encounter. Yet it is hardly likely that Pinkerton would have been so verdant as to have given his name.

The mail car was next plundered. Letters were cut open, one of which contained $2,000. The total booty obtained by the robbers reached about $11,500. When the robbers had effected their work, they released Alford and ordered the engineer to proceed with the train, which he did at once. They then mounted their horses and rode away in the darkness, and it is said that they rode sixty miles before they drew rein or gave themselves any rest. Then, putting up at the house of Hon. Mr. Mason, a member of the State Legislature, they demanded and obtained refreshments and rest.

The news of the robbery was, of course, telegraphed all along the line and an instant search was made. A **large body of well-armed men** tracked them a goodly distance. But the trail was lost. And in point of fact, hunting these robbers was a thankless task. No commensurate reward was ever offered. And hunting these men, as a skilful and traveled huntsman once said, was a good deal like hunting tigers. It was all very well when you were hunting the tiger, but when the tiger turned round and began to hunt you, it was another matter altogether.

Bentonville is a quiet little town in Benton county, Arkansas. One of the principal stores was kept by Thomas Craig & Son. This firm did a first-class business on a purely cash basis. On what was known as market day the country people from far and near would drive into Bentonville, and Craig & Son's store would be crowded until four or five o'clock.

On the afternoon of one of these market days—February 11th, 1874—between five and six o'clock, after a splendid day's business, Mr. Craig and his son were alone in the store, for at this time the country people were all well on their way home. The old gentleman was congratulating his son on the day's dealings, when all at once three strange-looking men entered the store.

"What can I do for you, gentlemen?" asked Mr. C⁓ig, senior, in his bland, polite manner, while h⁓

son Thomas came down from the desk to help serve the strange customers.

"You can keep quiet," was the blunt answer of the foremost of the men as he presented a revolver in each hand and continued: "If either of you speak a word or stir an inch, I'll blow your brains out, so if you value your d——d lives, why be quiet!"

Looking round the Craigs saw two other men keeping guard at the door. Resistance was utterly impossible. The safe door was open; it was the work of a moment to rifle it of its contents. But the robbers were disappointed. They expected to make a big haul, but the Craigs had banked all their cash on hand at four o'clock, and the safe only contained about $150. This greatly disgusted the rogues, so they swept up about $200 worth of valuable silks and went as quickly as they came, leaving strict charge that if they attempted to raise an alarm before they had time to leave the town, they would shoot them dead at sight.

It was quite clear that there was a well-organized raiding confederacy, but of whom did this confederacy consist?

There were, to start with, the Jameses, Frank and Jesse, and the Younger brothers. Ol Shepherd was dead, shot dead because he would not surrender to the representatives of the law. His brother, George W. Shepherd, one of the old followers of Quantrell, had settled down after the war and was married, and lived in Chaplin, Nelson county, Kentucky. After the raid on the Russelville bank he was arrested, tried, convicted and sentenced to a term of three years in the penitentiary. He left his wife at Chaplin in a house on which he had paid $600 purchase money. On his return from the penitentiary he found that his amiable wife, tiring of her loneliness, had made good use of the time, had obtained a divorce and was again married, having brought a new husband to the old house at Chaplin. This arrangement took Mr. Shepherd a little aback. But he looked at the circumstances a little, and then treated the whole affair most philosophically. Why should he disturb, or attempt to disturb, these happy relations? The cat had been away, the mice would play. So he left them to their own sweet wills and returned to his life of recklessness and shame, and there can be little doubt that George W. Shepherd was one of the boldest of this gang of desperadoes.

CHAPTER IX.

R   RY OF THE GATE RECEIPTS ON THE KANSAS CITY FAIR GROUNDS.

It was the great day of the Fair, the "big day" of the Kansas City Exposition. From early morning there had been a din of drum and trumpet and gong. Thousands upon thousands had poured in from all quarters. Leavenworth and Sedalia, St. Joseph and Moberly, Lawrence and Clinton and regions futher removed had sent in their crowded trains. All went merry as a marriage bell.

There were twenty thousand people on the fair ground that September afternoon, and thirty thousand more were crowding and surging up and down the streets of Kansas City.

One of the special features of that afternoon's entertainment was the races. Ethan Allen was to trot against a running mate at five o'clock. The people were crowding into the fair ground between four and five in masses. The ticket-sellers and the gatemen were doing a roaring trade. Mr. Hall, the secretary and treasurer of the association, had counted up the receipts of the day and found the same reached nearly $10,000 in hard cash. Arrangements had been made to bank this money at the First National Bank, though it was considerably after banking hours.

Mr. Hall called one of his trusty assistants and gave him a tin box containing the money, and sent him to deposit it in the bank according to arrangement. The idea of this box being stolen in a street crowded with tens of thousands of people was never dreamed of. It would have been regarded as quite preposterous to think anyone would have the daring to attempt so wild an exploit. The young man who had charge of this box started off, carrying the treasure in his right hand.

Just at this moment the general attention was arrested by the clatter of hoofs. Seven well-armed horsemen rode along, among whom, it is now universally believed, were Frank and Jesse James and Bob Younger. Their dress and manner were such that some of the more credulous spectators thought that this was a part of the show, and that the management had arranged for these "mummers" or "cowhellians" as part of the provided entertainments.

They were not kept long in doubt. The strange company dashed along, the crowd making way for them. One little girl was within a hair's breadth of being trampled to death. In a moment Jesse James sprang from his horse, drew his pistol and held it before the face of the luckless bearer of the treasure, while he snatched the box from his astonished grasp; and before either the cashier or the gaping crowd could take in the situation, the daring robber had remounted his horse, and the whole gang, with cocked pistols pointed at the people, and swearing instant death to any who dared to interfere with them, swept away as swift and as mysterious as a whirlwind. Not a shot was fired, not a life was lost. Ten thousand dollars, not in bills and bonds, but in hard cash!

"Clean work!" said one of the robbers to his comrades with a shrill whistle, as they counted the spoils.

For even these plunderers preferred money unstained by blood, if they could so obtain it. But money they would have, and if blood stood in the way, then blood must flow.

A more daring deed than this theft of the cashbox at Kansas City Fair the annals of crime does not present. The compeers and comrades of these wild raiders expressed their views of the whole affair in terse but suggestive language.

"The job was beautifully done," they said.

When the robbers had escaped—when the horse was gone!—the horse in this case being the cash-box—then there was much ado about fastening the stable door. The management of the Fair, the magistrates, authorities, the sheriffs, the marshals, the constables, big-wigs, little-wigs and bald-heads all turned out to shout after the lost horse and look well to the fastenings of said stable door.

Then there was hurrying and scurrying and hot pursuit. Over hill and over dale, by mountain and valley. The constables raged and the marshals swore. But raging and swearing were all in vain. The robbers rode five miles out of the city, broke open the tin box, counted and divided the "swag," then hanging the box from the limb of a tree, as a daring sarcastic relic of their visit to Kansas City, they parted—Frank and Jesse James to their friends in Jackson county; Bob and Cole Younger to Monegaw Springs, where they became the guests of a gentleman rejoicing in the name of Theodoric Snuffer.

The running of Ethan Allan was very tame that afternoon. Kansas City was in a doleful mood at the end of its great fair day. The hunters of the robbers came back vowing what they would have done if they had caught the miscreants; but the miscreants they caught not. They were willing enough to cook the hare in the most approved fashion. but, alas! the hare was not caught!

With the booty gathered from this daring feat the bandits were put in good financial position.

CHAPTER X.

KILLING OF JOHN YOUNGER AND TWO PINKERTON DETECTIVES.

The daring Gadshill robbery created a widespread consternation. There was not only danger for those who lived in the neighborhood of the haunts of these robbers, but if trains were to be boarded and every passenger robbed and threatened with death by men who always kept their dark vows to the very letter, who was safe? The whole community became thoroughly aroused, and it was determined at all costs and risks to have these robbers hunted and caught.

Allan Pinkerton was engaged by the Express Company. The whole force of detectives was greatly interested and not a little excited. There was money to be earned and a great reputation to be made if they succeeded in capturing these enemies of peace and order. The Secret Service force of the United States Government was ready to march at a moment's notice, the police and constabulary of Missouri and Arkansas were under orders. Everything pointed in the direction of success.

One company went in search of the Youngers. John and James Younger were known to have returned to Roscoe, in St. Clair county. Their pocket-books were well filled from the Gadshill fray. The whole detective force of St. Clair county was out under the direction of Captain W. J. Allen, whose real name was Lull. Allen was one of Pinkerton's most trusted men. Ed. B. Daniels, of Osceola, acted as guide, and a shrewd detective of St. Louis, known as a "fly cop," and calling himself Wright, made up the party in search of the notorious Youngers.

The three just named—Daniels, Allen, alias Lull, and Wright—were out riding one morning, March 16th, 1874, near the house of Theodoric Snuffer, not far from Roscoe. They were conversing in a low tone of voice, calculating the probabilities of finding the Youngers either at Snuffer's or in Roscoe. They were startled by a more sudden acquaintance with the Youngers than they had anticipated. John and James Younger had seen them from the window of Snuffer's house, and instead of hiding or seeking to escape they boldly determined to go out and meet them and dare them to do their worst. So, making a short detour, they overtook these searching men on the Chalk Level road. By this time Wright had left his companions and ridden ahead. Approaching Lull and Daniels from the rear, the elder of the brothers called out in a commanding tone of voice:

"Halt! Hold up your hands!" At the same time the two brothers presented their double-barrel shotguns full at the breasts of their would-be captors.

"You d——d dectectives, you thought you were not known," said Jim. "Now drop your pistols this moment, or, by G—d, we'll fire on you."

Without a moment's delay the detectives dropped their pistol belts in the road. James Younger then dismounted, having his brother John to keep their foes at bay with his gun while he secured the weapons that had just been thrown down at his command.

For a moment John, for some inconceivable reason, lowered his gun. That act sealed his doom. Captain Lull took advantage of the moment and fired from a revolver which he had concealed in his bosom. The shot took deadly effect in John Younger's neck, severing the carotid artery. With a wild yell and the look of a demon John fired a fatal retort to his adversary, and John Younger and Captain Lull both fell dead from their horses in the same moment. Daniels fired at James from a concealed revolver; a slight flesh wound was the result. James, half mad with pain and desperate at the sight of his dead brother, rushed like a tiger after Daniels, who was making for the woods. He sent a bullet crashing through his neck, and had the felicity of seeing him fall dead from his horse. Wright, the St. Louis "fly cop," had dashed ahead at the first cry of "Halt!" and had so spared his precious life.

James was in an uncontrolable agony because of his dead brother. He madly kissed his cold, blood-stained form, and swore that he would have a life for every drop of John's blood. He took the pistols John had used in so many fatal frays, and leaving to his friend Theodoric Snuffer the charge of John's funeral, he rode away, sad and solitary and brooding vengeance to the house of a well-tried friend in Boone county, Arkansas, there to plan future acts.

Such was the tragic end of the hunt for the Youngers.

John W. Wicher, of Chicago, was one of Pinkerton's best men. He was scarcely thirty years old, and yet he had won a reputation amongst the brave and daring as one of the coolest of them all. He was never excited, never in a hurry; but once set to a task

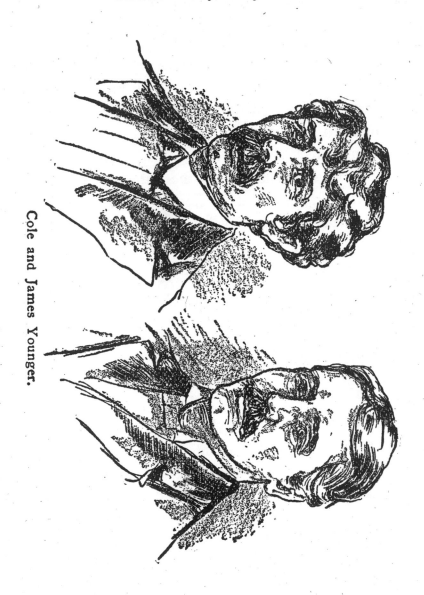

Cole and James Younger.

he followed it calmly and doggedly to the end. **Mr.**
William Pinkerton regarded Wicher as one of his
most reliable and accomplished men. In any dangerous enterprise he would have selected Wicher as the
most suitable man for a difficult and daring part.

Early in March, 1874, it was pretty well known that
the James boys and others of the gang of robbers
were in the neighborhood of Kearney, Clay county,
Missouri. Indeed, it was believed that a number of
them were staying at the house of Dr. Samuels.
Being made aware of this, Wicher formed the determination to go and arrange for the capture of the
gang, or at least of the ringleaders. Accordingly, on
the 10th of March he entered the office of his chief
in Chicago and asked permission to start on his perilous journey. What plans Wicher had formed in his
own mind will never be fully known. Mr. Pinkerton
pointed out to his assistant the dangers before him,
and from the first was reluctant to give his consent.
So many brave men had fallen before the deadly bullets of these miscreants that it seemed like running a
terrible risk to go out single-handed in search of their
whereabouts; and of all men Wicher was the last he
wanted to lose. After a very long deliberation he consented, and on the following day the brave detective

left his young wife and happy home to enter on that last fatal enterprise.

Wicher went straight to Liberty, the county town of Clay county, some twelve or fourteen miles from Kearney, the home of Dr. Samuels. He first visited the Commercial Savings Bank, where he made certain deposits and made the object of his visit known to Mr. Adkins, the president of the bank, who, while applauding his purpose, still was by no means sanguine of the result.

"You little know what you are daring," said the bank president, who was just as anxious as anybody that this robber band should be broken up. "I tell you a gang of devils would not be worse to meet than this crowd of blood-thirsty scoundrels who are led by Frank and Jesse James."

Liberty was a small town, and a stranger would be sure to be noticed if he stayed long. There was an eye on the wary detective more wary than his own. Jim Latche, fully aware that the hunt was up for his friends, the Jameses, noted the stranger at the bank. Something in his manner aroused suspicion, and Jim Latche watched with keen and ceaseless attention. From the bank he went to the house of Ex-Sheriff Moss, little dreaming that he was being followed and

watched. It was in vain that Mr. Moss urged him to
return. He gave him a terrible account of the prowess of the desperadoes; told him of their shrewdness
and of their merciless nature when excited by the
presence of an enemy, and warned him that he need
not hope to secure such wary men by strategem.
Colonel Moss was earnest in his efforts to dissuade
Wicher from making the rash attempt, but all en-
treaties were in vain. Wicher had started out and he
would not return without having made a trial. He
determined to assume the role of a tramp and apply
for farm work. Before he left Liberty he changed
his clothes for those of a farm laborer. Latche saw
this, and this was enough. Away he sped to Kearney
and gave Jesse James timely warning.

Never did man walk more deliberately into his
grave than did Detective Wicher that bright spring
afternoon. Jesse James, Jim Anderson and Bradley
Collins were all on the alert. The afternoon train
brought Wicher to Kearney, and without suspicion of
danger he went towards the Samuels homestead. The
three desperadoes, who had resolved on their course
of action, were hiding by the roadside. When near
Dr. Samuels' home, Jesse suddenly confronted the
somewhat astonished Wicher.

"Good evening, sir," said Wicher.

"Where in h—ll are you going?" responded the other.

"I am seeking work. Can you tell me where I can get some work on a farm?"

"No, not much; you don't want any, either, you d—— thief! Old Pinkerton has already given you a job that will last you as long as you live, I reckon."

Wicher was taken aback, but he soon took in the whole situation. In a moment Jesse's pistol was brought to sight, and he laughed that scornful laugh that has no mercy in its tone. Wicher was not greatly perturbed, but saw at once that the only possible chance was conciliation. That was the last card in his hand, but he played it in vain.

"Well, this is a singular adventure, I declare," said Wicher. "Now, why you make such a mistake concerning me is more than I can imagine. You are surely making sport of me. I tell you I know nothing of the persons of whom you speak, and why should you interrupt me? Let me go on, for I must find a place to stop tonight, anyhow."

Jesse James laughed outright. "What," said he, "were you doing at Liberty today? Why did you deposit money in the bank? What business did you have

with Adkins and Moss? Where are the clothes you
wore? Plotting to capture the James boys, eh?" and
Jesse laughed aloud, and Jim Anderson and Fox and
another confederate of the boys came from their con-
cealment with pistols in hand. Poor Wicher saw this,
and for the first time he fully realized the helplessness
of his position.

Then Jesse James added in a merciless, swearing
tone of voice: "Young man, we want to hear no more
from you. We know you. Move but a finger and
you die now. Boys," he said, addressing Anderson
and Fox, "I don't think it best to do the job here. It
wouldn't take long, but for certain reasons I don't
think this is the place. Shall we cross the river tonight?" The others answered they would if it was
his pleasure.

All this time Wicher stood calm and silent. He was
consciously facing the inevitable. At a command from
Jesse his pistol was taken from him; and in the midst
of their grim sport one of the boys, on examining
Wicher's hands, said:

"Damned fine hands these for the hands of a farm
laborer. You've not done much farm work of late,
my beauty! But you've done all the work you'll ever
do for Pinkerton or anybody else, my dear sir!"

The plans of the bandits were complete. Wicher was disarmed, and now he was bound by strong cords and a gag put in his mouth to keep him from raising an alarm.

Later on in the evening he was put upon a horse, his legs firmly tied under the horse's belly. Jesse James, Jim Anderson and Bradley Collins followed, making up an awful procession. On they went, hour after hour, and the wretched man, gagged and bound, had his ears regaled with the detailed plan of his execution.

By three o'clock next morning they reached Blue Mills, on the Mississippi River, woke up the sleepy ferryman, and, under the pretense that they were on the track of horse thieves, they persuaded him to take them across the river. The ferryman obeyed, and, making some sort of gruff reference to the man who was gagged, they told him that he was one of the captured thieves. They had crossed the river, and in a dark copse in Jackson county the dreadful deed of murder was wrought.

Wicher was taken from the horse on which he had ridden his last sad ride and bound to a tree. The gag was taken out of his mouth, and then by a process of slow, awful torture the wretched demons sought to extract from him some information concerning the plans of Pinkerton. But it was in vain. Wicher saw that death was before him, and he determined not to speak. They cut and slashed him with their bowie-knives; they dragged his head down till his neck was nearly broken; but all was in vain; and when at last they saw that no amount of torture would induce him to speak, they finished their ghastly work. And amid sneer and jest and ribald taunt they sent one bullet crashing through his brain and another through his heart.

So ended the tragedy of Wicher's fruitless search.

Captain Lull, Edward Daniels and John W. Wicher had fallen victims before the men they went out to capture. A thousand mingling emotions stirred the minds of the public at large on the tidings of these shameful murders. But in the minds of Pinkerton and the whole detective force there was a bitter sense of humiliation mingling with sincere regret.

CHAPTER XI.

DASTARDLY CRIME OF THE PINKERTON DETECTIVES.

A detective campaign was organized that was to put an end forever to the outrages of these wily brigands. William Pinkerton, a brother of the chief detective, was sent to Kansas City with five of the most trusted men of the force. All the plans were to be well and carefully laid, nothing was to be left to chance. Constant communication in cypher was kept with Chicago. As soon as Pinkerton arrived in Kansas City the sheriff of Clay county was sent for, and it became abundantly clear that the detectives could reckon upon the sympathy and moral support of a very large proportion of the best citizens of the county. A careful watch was set about the Samuels homestead, in which twelve trusty citizens were engaged, and reports were furnished hour by hour. It was arranged that none of the detectives were to be in the neighborhood of Kearney till the time had come to strike the decisive blow, the day for which was

fixed January 25th, 1875. That cold wintry afternoon
Frank and Jesse James were both seen in the front
yard of the Samuels residence. Of this fact there is
no doubt for a single moment. The fact that they
were there was telegraphed to Pinkerton; it was believed that the two young men would spend the evening under their mother's roof. It was, therefore, resolved under cover of the night to assault the house,
which had long been called "Castle James," and secure
both Frank and Jesse.

But Frank and Jesse were never without friends,
and there can be little doubt that the whole scheme of
Pinkerton had been communicated to the brothers.
Whether there had been any betrayal of trust on the
part of anyone, or whether the schemers had been
outschemed by some cunning secret friends of the
boys, or whether a sort of devil's luck had made the
boys restless, it is hard to tell. They had keen noses
for a scent, and they may have smelt that there was
danger in the air. Be this as it may, soon after night-
fall on this memorable 25th of January, when all ar-
rangements for their capture were perfected, when
squads and posses of detectives and private citizens
were drawing a cordon round the ill-fated house,
when a special train was on its way from Kansas City

to Kearney with a large force to "make assurance doubly sure," Frank and Jesse saddled their horses, bade their respected parents a tender farewell and quickly rode away, without hindrance or molestation. None of the vigilant guards saw them depart, and when the hour fixed on for the attack came they were fifty miles away, quietly enjoying the evening in the house of a friend.

The assaulting party had no information that the birds had flown, but quietly and confidently they were drawing nearer and nearer to the house, sure as they thought of their prey, and determined to take them dead or alive.

At the hour of midnight the attack began. Nine well-armed men from Pinkerton's force led the attack. Balls of tow saturated in coal oil and turpentine were carried along, and two heavy hand grenades with a 32-pound shell. It was not without some fear that they marched to the attack. There had been so many surprises of terror that to be met by a fierce and murderous repulse would only have been in keeping with the past history of the Jameses.

Two of the attacking party approached a window on the west side of the house, and in attempting to open it woke an old colored woman who had been for years a servant of the family. She gave an alarm at once. But the window was forced open and two balls of fire were thrown into the apartment. This brought all the inmates of the house in terror to this strange, unexpected scene. There were in the house Dr. and Mrs. Samuels, Miss Susie Samuels and some younger children. Instantly the room was filled with smoke and flame. The plan was to arrest Frank and Jesse the moment they should appear upon the scene, as was supposed they would be sure to do on the first sight of the threatening fire. All around the house were detectives and citizens with cocked pistols ready to challenge the boys to surrender, and if they would not to make an end of their miserable lives.

The young children screamed and wailed most piteously. Mrs. Samuels, true to her stern nature, began issuing commands and doing all that was possible to subdue the fire. Then followed a dastardly and shameful piece of business. One of the detectives flung a hand grenade into the room amongst the terrified women and screaming children. A dreadful explosion followed, and then screams of anguish and groans as of the dying. But the brigands made no sign. For the best of all reasons—they were fifty miles away.

The attacking party being pretty well satisfied by this time that neither Frank nor Jesse were there, and without waiting to see the result of their onslaught, turned their steps homeward. A more cowardly and ignoble ending of a carefully laid plot can scarcely be imagined. The hurling of that hand grenade was beyond all things wanton and cruel, and altogether unworthy of men with any sense of honor.

When the consternation within had somewhat subsided, Dr. Samuels lit a lamp, and there before him was a scene that utterly beggars description. There lay their little eight-year-old son in the agonies of a painful death. The exploding shell had completely torn the boy's side away. Mrs. Samuels lay in a pool of blood, her left arm shattered and hanging helpless by her side. Susie and the poor old servant were both bleeding from desperate wounds. The scene was horrible. There was blood everywhere, and agonies and groans, and in the pale glimmer of the flickering lamplight the poor boy turned his pale face to his mother and with a great cry of anguish died.

It was a terrible night, that 25th of January, 1875! There was blundering and bungling on the one hand, and the most unwarrantable cruelty on the other. If

Frank and Jesse had been home there would probably
have been a very different record.

Years after, when someone asked Mrs. Samuels if
Frank or Jesse were really home that night, she looked
a very stern look at her questioner and said:

"Do you suppose that either Frank or Jesse would
have been there and nobody killed?"

The funeral of the slaughtered child took place on
the 28th of January. Mrs. Samuels had had her arm.
amputated and was not able to attend the funeral.
But a great crowd attended the funeral, and that little
coffin laid under the winter snow wrought a great
change in the feelings of the citizens of Clay county.

Mr. Daniel H. Askew was a flourishing farmer and
a much respected gentleman living near the Samuels'
residence, in Clay county. His opinion as to the whole
family living under Dr. Samuels' roof was anything
but flattering. And he was one of those men who did
not hesitate to give utterance to his views. He was
believed to be a member of the posse which made the
shameful attack on Castle James on that sad January
night. Albeit, he himself declared again and again
that he had no share or part in Pinkerton's raid.
Still, for reasons best known to themselves, Frank
and Jesse James both held Askew to be one of their

inveterate foes, and felt persuaded from evidence they had obtained that Dan Askew had led the detective gang that had brought death and desolation to their home.

On the night of April 12th, 1875, and about 8 o'clock in the evening, Mr. Askew went to a spring, about fifty yards from his house, for a bucket of water. It was moonlight, bright and clear. He returned from the spring, set the bucket on the porch, and was just in the act of taking a drink of the cool spring water, when three shots rang out in the still moonlit air, and the ill-fated gentleman fell dead on his face on the porch of his home with three bullets in his brain. The wife and the daughter of the murdered man rushed out just in time to see three men come from the corner of the woodpile, mount their horses and ride swiftly away.

Who killed Dan Askew?

That question can, perhaps, be never fully answered. There is very little doubt that the three men were Frank and Jesse James and Clell Miller; for a little later, the same night, three men answering to the above named, as far as could be well discovered in the moonlight, called at the house of Mr. Henry Sears and summoned him to the door and said:

"See here, we have killed Dan Askew, and if any of his friends want to know who did the job, tell them detectives did it."

Without a single scrap more evidence, the public concluded in their own minds that Frank and Jesse were the perpetrators of this last murder, and the tide that had turned in their favor was beginning to flow back into its old channel.

After the death of Mr. Askew, the bandits, fearing a general rising against them—for Mr. Askew was a general favorite throughout the whole district of Western Missouri—thought it best to relieve the State of their presence for a little while, and, besides, funds running low, it was felt desirable to seek for the replenishment of their resources in greener fields and pastures new.

Accordingly, after having spent a little time in the Indian Territory, they resolved to journey into Texas and try their luck among the rangers of that wild prairie region. The select company of robbers whose exploits are now to be recorded was composed of the redoubtable Jesse James, Clell Miller, Jim Reed and Cole and Jim Younger, and another of the lawless band, probably Frank James. After a brief council of war, they agreed on robbing the mail that runs between San Antonio and Austin. They determined upon a spot on the highway about twenty-three miles southwest of Austin, and there lay in peaceful ambush awaiting the arrival of the stage coach.

CHAPTER XII.

ROBBERY OF THE SAN ANTONIO AND AUSTIN STAGE COACH AND THE KANSAS PACIFIC RAILROAD NEAR DENVER.

On the day of the robbery of the San Antonio and Austin stage the passengers were the Right Rev. Bishop Gregg, of the Protestant Episcopal Diocese of Texas; Mr. Breckenridge, president of the First National Bank of San Antonio, and other ladies and gentlemen of good standing—eleven in all. Merry, happy souls, who knew the brighter side of life, and knew no lack of earthly gear. The stage called at its usual halting place about six o'clock in order that man and beast might be refreshed.

Just after resuming their journey the driver descried ahead of him six mounted men, whom he took for rancheros; but as they drew nearer he became a little puzzled. They were mounted not on the rough mustang of the prairies, but on splendid American horses of the best breed. The driver became a little anxious, and said, half to himself, in language more expressive than grammatical:

"Them's queer fellers, I'll swear. I don't much like the looks on 'em."

His fears were soon realized. The foremost of the mounted gang, presenting a loaded pistol, cried out in a voice of thunder:

"Halt! D——n your soul, halt, or I'll blow your brains out!"

Poor old Tony Weller never wished for an alibi for the immortal Pickwick half as earnestly as this San Antonio coachman wished for an alibi for himself in that unhappy moment. Of course, he obeyed the command, and in less time than it takes to tell the six robbers—three on each side—held the whole company of the stage under cover of their pistols.

"Come, tumble out!" was the brief command. "Tumble out quick, if you don't want to die where you sit."

A scene of confusion ensued. The women of the party lost all presence of mind, and without the slightest regard for the proprieties clambered over and clung to the gentlemen of the party for protection. Surely, never in this world, was a bishop hugged on the broad highway as that bishop was hugged by a

very ponderous maiden lady, of a very certain age, as
she begged him for the love of God to protect her
from "those wicked, horrd men."

But the bishop was more in danger than his stout-
clinging friend.   Indeed, there was little danger to the
women of the company, if they would but keep quiet.
Jesse James did most of the talking on the occasion,
though Younger occasionally put in a word. The ladies
were assured they had nothing to fear, if only the
men behaved themselves. "Behaving themselves" on
this occasion meant simply getting out of the stage
and delivering all their possessions quietly.

"Come, tumble out or die!" was Jesse's brief command.

None of the company wanted to die, not even the
bishop.   Heaven was no doubt much better than
Texas, but they all preferred Texas for the present.
They hoped to go to heaven in the distant future, but
just then they preferred San Antonio to Paradise,
even though they should get there with empty pockets.
So the gentlemen tumbled out, and were ranged in a
row, two of the robbers keeping guard with cocked
pistols, while the others searched the baggage.   After
plundering the trunks and boxes of the passengers,
they turned their attention to the United States mail

bags, from which a large sum of money was extracted. And now came the plunder of personal possessions.

"Gentlemen and ladies," said Jesse in a mock politeness, "it will be our painful duty now to trouble you for the money and jewelry you may chance to have about you."

"Do you mean to rob us?" asked the bishop in a tone of offended dignity, as he gazed on the scene.

"Oh! fie, fie," said the shocked young robber; "you shouldn't use such ugly language! Rob you! Oh! never, never! We would scorn the action! Do we look like robbers? No, gentlemen, we only wish to relieve you of a burden—that's all, old sock; so out with your money and quick, we have no time to spare."

"Don't you call that robbery?" asked the bishop.

"Come, now, old coon! Dry up, or you'll not have an opportunity to ask any more nonsensical questions. Hand out your money."

The bishop reluctantly complied, handing out his pocketbook.

"Now that watch of yours!" Jesse further commanded.

"What! Will you not allow me to keep my watch? It is a gift and dearly prized. You would not rob an humble minister of Christ of his timepiece, would you?" queried the bishop, in plaintive tones.

"Hand over that watch," said Jesse, growing impatient. "You must pay the full toll."

"You would not rob a minister of the gospel of a cherished gift, would you?" he asked most piteously.

"What! you are a parson, are you? A meek shepherd, are you? A poor, unworthy vessel!" said Jesse with a sneer. "So much the more reason you should pay. You have no need of a watch. Get you camel's-hair and that sort of thing."

Jesse's remembrances of the old days of his father's struggling ministry were revived. He remembered the hard conflict his father had with pecuniary difficulties. He had often heard stories of that hard fight and he had no large place of sympathy for well-to-do, well-clad, sleek ecclesiastics. So he taunted the bishop further:

"Look here, my reverend old buck, Jesus Christ didn't have any watch, and He didn't ride in stages, either. He walked about to do His Father's will, and wasn't arrayed in fine clothes, and didn't fare sumptuously every day. What use has a' preacher for a watch? Go and travel like the Master. Out with that watch! No more words—not one, mind you! We are not Christians, we are Philistines."

Most reluctantly the bishop gave up the valuable timepiece, which he valued above all price as the gift of loved and trusting friends.

"If you've anything more, out with it and quick, I'm wasting time," cried Jesse, growing angry, in real earnest.

The bishop decared that he had not; but Cole Younger thought it better that he should be searched, urging as the argument for such a proceeding that "you could never trust these d——d canting Christians in an affair of honor." The bishop submitted to the search with a groan, but nothing of value being found on him, he was let go.

The eight gentlemen were all searched, but very little was obtained till they came to Mr. Breckenridge, of the San Antonio Bank. He proved to be a big bonanza. They obtained from him over $1,000. The ladies were ordered to yield up their treasures. One was old and evidently poor. They examined her pocketbook, and Jesse said:

"Madam, is that all you have?"

"Every cent I have in the world," she replied.

"And how far are you going?"

"To Houston, sir."

"Well, then, take your money; we won't trouble you."

To her intense surprise, the affrighted old lady found, when she got home, that Jesse had slipped a twenty-dollar bill into her poorly furnished pocketbook, and she was wont to say in after years:

"Well, well, the boys were bad enough, Heaven knows, but they might have been a good deal worse."

From the other two ladies they took their possessions. From the fat old maid who had clasped the bishop to her throbbing breast they took a valuable gold watch and about a hundred dollars in cash.

They were nearly two hours at their task, but they were never molested, and not one of that company offered any sign of resistance. They made a haul of about $3,500. They took the lead span of horses, enjoined strict silence and secrecy on those whom they had robbed, and then rode away into the dark and silent night.

The San Antonio stage rumbled on, a sad, dispirited and poverty-stricken party. They were all of them philosophers enough to see that things might have been much worse. They had saved their lives at the cost of their possessions, and on the whole they settled down to the view that they might have made a much worse bargain.

Shortly after this robbery it came to the knowledge of the gang that the government intended to send a large shipment of gold dust eastward from Denver by the Kansas Pacific Railroad. There can be little doubt that some of these robbers had friends somewhere among the railway or mint agents; but if they had, the secret was well kept. Anyway, the robbers knew that there was to be a very large shipment at a certain date, not long hence, so from Texas the boys journeyed northward through the Indian Territory to Kansas.

About six miles from Kansas City, in Wyandotte county, is a little wayside station called Muncie—a quiet little station all alone in the hills, with no dwelling place for miles around. There was a large water tank there where the train generally stayed for water. But for this fact, and for its association with one of the most daring and successful of robberies, the name of Muncie might never have been heard. It was quite dark when the train reached Muncie station. As the train halted at the water tank there was a low, shrill whistle, and just a whispered word from Jesse:

"Now, boys! Quick, and quiet and steady!" That was all, and instantly the train was boarded. Bill Mc-

Daniels held the engineer and fireman under charge of two pistols, and swore if they as much as "winked any eyebrow" he would shoot them dead.

The robbers then rushed through the cars, commanding the passengers to keep their seats and be silent or death would be instantly their portion. Two of the band stood on the platform of the cars, with cocked pistols, keeping, each of them, guard on two doors. In the meantime the remaining three rushed to the baggage car. The express messenger was overpowered, and in less time than it takes to write the story the van was sacked, and the wild robbers in less than fifteen minutes had possessed themselves of thirty thousand dollars' worth of gold dust, and silver and other valuables to the extent of $25,000 more, and were riding away into the dark winter's night.

They had stolen in that brief space of time, without the slighest effort at resistance, *fifty-five thousand dollars!* and not one cent of that huge sum was ever got back again, nor were one of the robbers ever arrested on the charge of complicity in this affair.

Of course they were vigorously pursued, and of course they were not caught! And, after all, there is no great wonder. It was a good deal safer to put their heads in a lion's mouth than to be found within range

of the unerring pistols of the Jameses, or the Youngers, or the desperate Clell Miller!

Some days after Bill McDaniels was arrested in
Kansas City for being drunk, and there was found
in his possession a sheepskin bag and a large sum of
money. These he swore he had honestly earned in
Colorado. But these possessions looked very suspicious, and he was removed to Lawrence, Kansas, to
await his trial—the ill-fated Lawrence that Quantrell
and his band so utterly destroyed when the old black
flag was flying, and Jim Lane and his Jayhawkers had
to be avenged. Con O'Hara, a clever detective, was
detailed to pump Bill and get him to squeal about the
Muncie affair. But Con's hydraulic powers failed.

"Did he budge?" said O'Hara's chief.

"Divil a bit!" said Con. "Coaxing and threatening,
it was all the same; he was as ignorant as a pig and
as dumb as Ailsa Craig!"

Being taken from the calaboose at Lawrence for
trial, Bill managed to escape, and for a whole week
he was hiding in the woods.

A posse was formed and Bill was hunted down
with bloodhounds. One of the posse rashly rushed
in upon the fugitive, meeting a terrible fate, Mc-

Daniels stabbing him to death with a vicious Bowie knife. But the day of reckoning had arrived, for as he was making a dash for liberty a powerful bloodhound sprang at his throat, whilst a shot from the timber ploughed its way through his breast just as another member of the posse approached knife in hand, ready to finish the career of the noted guerrilla. But even in death he was true to his partners in guilt, and would not divulge a single name or clue to make plain the mystery of Muncie's successful raid.

The robber gang was highly incensed at Bill McDaniels for allowing himself to be taken, and to be taken drunk, but after his fidelity, even in death, they wiped out the memory of his folly; and sitting one night soon after in their safe retreat, they spoke of him only what they thought was praiseworthy. If it had been a genuine Irish wake, they could not have been more profuse in their compliments, and as the night went on

> "Each one said
> Something good of the boy who was dead."

And, last of all, Jesse charged his comrades to fill a bumper, and half-grimly, half-sadly said:

"D——n it, boys, he was a brick, after all, so here's

A powerful bloodhound sprang at his throat.

to Bill McDaniels, *wherever he is,*" added Jesse, with a strange, half-solemn look. "He was game to the last and died without a squeal! Here's to Bill!"

CHAPTER XIII.

THE HUNTINGDON RAID AND THE MISSOURI - PACIFIC RAILROAD ROBBERY.

Huntingdon is a small town in the hills of Western Virginia, on the Ohio River, in Cabell county, and is on the line of the Chesapeake and Ohio Railroad. The opening of the railway had given the little town of 3,000 inhabitants a new life, and the sleepy streets became quite animated by the vigor of a new commercial life. The bank of Huntingdon was doing a brisk little business, and Mr. R. T. Oney, the cashier, was widely respected by all the citizens of the thriving little town.

It was two o'clock in the afternoon. Suddenly four men, well mounted, rode up Huntingdon street. They excited no attention; they made no special sign. Arrived at the bank, two of them dismounted and entered the bank. These were Frank James and Cole Younger. They covered the cashier and his customer with two pistols, assuring them that their one chance for life was to keep quiet. The safe door was open. Ten thousand dollars in ready cash were speedily rolled into a bag brought for that purpose. With more threats, and with the assurance that to sound an alarm would only be to ring their own funeral knell, the robbers mounted their horses and fled away to the fastnesses of the Virginia hills. Half an hour had sufficed for this romantic transaction! Time was not money to the robbers—it was more, it was life! In thirty minutes they had gained $10,000. They could hardly have made it quicker in Wall street or at the Chicago Board of Trade!

As the robbers rode away they saw the citizens were beginning to understand the state of affairs, and as they went they kept firing right and left to intimidate any who might be disposed to stay their progress.

Before an hour had passed away the Sheriff, at the head of twenty-five citizens, set out in hot pursuit. The authorities of other counties were notified, and very soon the whole of that region became a hunting ground. Bligh, the St. Louis detective, was largely directing the search. Away the robbers sped into the hills and hiding places of Eastern Kentucky and Tennessee. A hundred miles away from Huntingdon the man-hunters sighted their prey. A parley was called and a terrific fight ensued. The runaways had been

compelled to abandon their horses. In the fray a
bullet found its way to Tom McDaniel's heart and
stopped forever its wild pulsations.

That hunt lasted four weeks. Jack Keen was captured in Fentress county, Tennessee, lodged in Cabell
jail, and afterwards sentenced to eight years' imprison-
ment in the penitentiary, where he still resides.

The two leaders, Frank James and Cole Younger,
were not captured; they escaped to the Indian Territory. The spoils not having been yet divided, the two
successful robbers bagged $5,000 each.

So ended the Huntingdon raid.

After the escape from the Huntingdon raid Frank
met his brother Jesse in the Indian Territory, and so
far from being dismayed, they seemed to be only
encouraged to further wild adventures. The perils
that would have filled timid minds with fear and dread
seemed to be to these boys a perfect inspiration. They
were playing a high game, they had made great hauls,
and the glitter of the gold made them disposed to
underestimate the perils that thickened about them and
increased with every wild raid.

A long and carefully prepared plot was now arranged for the wrecking of an express train. The
gang was increasing. but this increase was not without

some disadvantages. The larger number became unwieldly in management, the chances of arousing suspicion were greater, the chances of capture were increased, and when it came to the simplest of all questions—the dividing of the spoils—then it was found much easier to divide $10,000 among four then seven. Still, this gang set themselves to their perilous task— Bill Longley, Sam Bass, the Haskins and Moores of the Indian Territory, and last of all, Hobbs Kerry, a Texan ranger, who had all the wickedness but none of the pluck and endurance necessary to make a first-class villain. Kerry was never fit for any dangerous post, and the wonder is that he gained admission to the gang at all. He never did anything but hold the horses of the robbers, and when caught at last by his own drunken folly he gave his comrades shamefully away. The point determined on for this daring robbery was a little spot known as Rocky Cut, about four miles east of Otterville, in Pettis county, Missouri. At this Rocky Cut a huge bridge spanned the Lamine River, and a watchman was always kept in lonely guardianship of the bridge. The plan which so thoroughly succeeded was to capture the watchman, show the red light when the train approached, and then as the train stopped board it, rob the express car, and then fly for life.

All the plans were most carefully and thoroughly digested. Nothing was left to chance or peradventure. The plan had been largely concocted in the fertile brain of Frank James, but Jesse was undoubtedly the leading spirit of its execution.

The rendezvous was about two miles east of the Lamine River. By sundown the whole posse had arrived. Hushed and silent, they marched in that summer twilight, till they found within a hundred yards of the bridge a thick, dense copse crowded with trees in their richest foliage, and thick enough to be a safe and secure covert from all ordinary gaze. Here their horses were secured and left in charge of Bill Chadwell and Hobbs Kerry. It was now close upon nine o'clock. The business of securing the watchman was delegated to Clell Miller, Charlie Pitts and Bob Younger. Accordingly they went down to the bridge between nine and ten o'clock. The watchman, hearing footsteps, cried out with voice as full of astonishment as command:

"Hello! who's there? What do you want at this time o' night?"

With that he swung his lantern and stared into the faces of his late visitors, only to be terrified with the sight of a pair of heavy navy revolvers most uncomfortably near his venerable nose.

"What are you going to do with me?" asked the astonished watchman.

"You keep still, that's all you have to do," was the reply.

"But you ain't going to hurt me?" he inquired.

"What do we want to hurt you for? We want that money on the train, that's all we care for. So give up your lantern and come along and be quiet, and you'll be all right. But if you're fool enough to make a noise—why, lookee here!—smell o' that!" and with this piece of good advice Jesse put the muzzle of his revolver still nearer the old man's nose.

The old man had passed the age when a man must be either be a fool or a philosopher, and he had chosen the philosophic side, and therefore he gave everything up to the robbers, and seemed, indeed, much more disposed to oblige his late visitors than to cross or vex them. The poor old watchman was taken away into temporary captivity.

At a rocky cut the rails were loosened and obstructions placed upon the track. The red lantern of the watchman was prepared and concealed, to be used at the proper moment, and all lay waiting for the game that must certainly fall into the trap so simply laid.

All was now ready. The danger signal was to be

shown by Charlie Pitts. The robbers lay dow., in ambush, and scarcely spoke a word for nearly an hour.

At last the Missouri Pacific train, with its costly freight, came tearing along. The danger signal was hoisted, the train stopped and was immediately boarded by these masked robbers. The passengers were held in check by a robber at each door of the car, with loaded irons, threatening death if any of them should rise for one moment from their seats. It was now the uniform policy of the band to be satisfied with whatever was found in the express car. The robber guards, therefore, were free to promise the passengers that if they sat still they should go on their way unmolested. The leaders of the work of plunder compelled the express messengers, under threats of instant death, to open the safe. The contents were then emptied into a leather sack, without which the boys never traveled.

The shrill whistle of Jesse James indicated that the job was done. The train was ordered forward. The robbers seized every moment of time, mounted their horses and rode away into the darkness of that Missourian summer night.

The whole transaction had hardly taken the space of one brief hour, and the result was $17,000, besides jewelry and many valuables.

The robbers rode on in a southerly direction. The story of their bloodless exploit had been telegraphed all over the Western States. The detectives of St. Louis, Kansas City, Chicago, and even of the seaboard cities were all on the alert, but before the July sun rose on the morning of the 9th the robbers had ridden fifty miles, found a dark safe spot, where they divided the spoils, and adjourned *sine die*. They went away in couples, and for a' time there seemed no clue to the identity of the robbers, save only the common-sense clue, that only the Jameses and the Youngers were equal to such tasks—"Jesse James, his mark"—was pretty plain on all these border raids.

Not one of the band was taken save Hobbs Kerry, and he first of all gave himself utterly away. Hobbs had been all along half-rogue, whole beggar, hanging on to any skirts, dirty or clean, if it did but pay for the time. He finds himself now in unusual good luck. He had by a pure fluke, as far as he was concerned, come in for a big bonanza. The beggar was suddenly placed on horseback, and he took the usual ride.

Both the Jameses were worried about Hobbs Kerry. They didn't know him, and they were more than a little surprised that they had trusted him so far on so slight an acquaintance.

"If the cub should be caught they might make him squeal," said Frank, thoughtfully.

"Time enough to worry about that when he's caught and squeals!" answered Jesse, who left all the business of borrowing trouble to his more sedate elder brother.

At the same time even Jesse could not wholly disguise from himself that he felt a little nervous about the "cub."

Kerry had parted company from Pitts and Chadwell after fording the Grand River, and now flush with ready cash, he goes to Fort Scott, in Kansas, and there arrays himself in gorgeous array, and begins to play the "fast young gentleman," which is only another name for the "perfect fool." He visited Fort Scott, Vinita, Parsons, Granby and Joplin, and had a good time with the boys generally; and just as long as the "stamps" were on hand there were plenty of the boys ready to help him to have his good time. It was women and whisky and cards, alternating with whisky and cards and women! For about six weeks he had a "high old time." Bagnios, gambling hells, dance-houses, he squandered his ill-gotten money, and when the whisky was in he forgot to be mum. He was watched and betrayed.

Frank and Jesse James denounced him as a fraud, and declared all the story of the "danger signal" as born of a wild, mad brain; and for some time they were thoroughly believed by thousands in the Western States. They had still hundreds of friends, and thoroughly disinterested friends, too.

Large rewards were offered for the robbers of the train at Otterville. The whole economy of detective forces were at work; Missouri, Arkansas, Kentucky and the Indian Territory were scoured for months. But not a dollar of the stolen money was ever found nor one of the robbers caught, excepting Hobbs Kerry—the "cub."

At the time of which we are writing the detectives held Missouri, Arkansas, Texas, Kentucky and Iowa under a kind of surveillance, and with this fact the James boys were perfectly well acquainted. Their redoubtable mother—their trusty and ablest ally—rendered them most efficient assistance in this direction. And now, tiring of inaction, as they always did after a brief space of rest and revelry, they held a council of war, to which the notorious Bill Chadwell was invited. The council was held in a forest in Clay county, not far from the house of Dr. Samuels. The whole plans were submitted to Mrs. Samuels, and met with her approval. That strange, awful spiri. of hatred that possessed her prior to the midnight raid upon her home, when her darling boy was killed, Susie wounded and her own arm shattered, had grown in intensity. If she breathed vengeance against all detectives before, she now breathed vengeance doubly distilled. It was her boast, made over and over again:

"I hate all detectives as I hate the devil, and if I had my way I'd send them all where they belong before sundown!"

The reason for inviting Bill Chadwell, the notorious Minnesota horse-thief, to this council was to consult him as to the geographical characteristics of their new field of daring. In following his nefarious occupation Chadwell had been compelled to ride through all the region over which they proposed to extend their visits. It was arranged, after a long consultation, that Chadwell should act as guide through the new paths of peril that were destined to prove so fatal to the weird council which met in the light of the harvest moon under the sombre shadows of the Missouri forest. Chadwell had many friends who could be relied upon, if any danger came, to render assistance and shelter.

One of the motives that suggested that the outlaws should try their fortune in a northern direction was in order to utterly confuse the officers in pursuit of them. Moreover, the time was opportune. The grain growers were just disposing of their crops; the farmers were flush; there were plenty of funds in the banks, and the fact that Minnesota had heard of them only, and not seen them, and certainly had no anticipation of a visit from such illustrious adventurers, all seemed to speak in favor of the experiment.

The gang was made up of a double quartette of daring bravadoes. Frank and Jesse James, Coleman, Jim and Bob Younger, Charlie Pitts, Clell Miller and Bill Chadwell, the latter acting as guide.

The place for assault was a matter of debate. Cole Younger, as was afterwards believed, was moved by his "good angel"—for even these men believed in their good and bad angels—in opposing, for some inexplicable reason, the raid into Minnesota. He would have preferred Canada, and said that London, Toronto or Montreal, or even Kingston, the city of the Ontario Penitentiary, could by new and special methods be worked effectively. It was a law amongst the robbers that the majority in council ruled absolutely. Every one of them had the fullest opportunity of speech, but the vote once taken, there was no appeal, and every man threw himself into the scheme with all enthusiasm.

Mankato was first thought of, but Bill Chadwell had a friend at Mankato whose information pointed in the direction of Northfield as a more likely theatre for their daring drama.

The band of eight divided themselves and took different ways. On the 3d of September they met at Mankato and completed their plans of robbing the Northfield Bank. Their place of rendezvous was the house of one of Chadwell's warmest friends. They came and held their council unnoticed and unknown. All was quiet, and not the least suspicion was abroad that any robbery was contemplated.

CHAPTER XIV.

THE NORTHFIELD BANK ROBBERY—THE GANG COMES TO GRIEF.

Northfield, Minn., is a little town on the line of the Milwaukee and St. Paul Railroad, in the northeastern division of Rice county.

Just about noon three strangers on horseback came in from the north by the Dundas road and went and dined on the west side of the Cannon River, which flows through the village.

The bank building was in the chief block on the public square. After their dinner these three strangers—who were Frank and Jesse James and Coleman Younger—tied up their horses nearly in front of the bank, and after a brief chat, which seemed to be of a most important kind, they entered the bank. At this moment three fierce-looking men rode in mad haste over the east bridge into the village, yelling like demons, brandishing their revolvers and shooting wildly right and left, while two others came from the west in the same mad fashion, shooting out and commanding all people to go into their houses and keep quiet. Meantime a terrible tragedy was being transacted at the bank. The three brigands leapt over the counter and Frank James drew his knife and held it at the throat of Mr. J. L. Haywood, the cashier of the bank, demanding that he should at once open the safe.

"I will do no such thing," said the brave cashier.

"Quick now," said Jesse, "or you die like a dog!"

"I can't help that," said Mr. Haywood. "I will do my duty, if I die!"

"Then die," said Jesse, and in less than a moment a bullet went whizzing through the cashier's brain, and he fell instantly dead at his assassin's feet.

"You, here," said Cole Younger to Mr. A. E. Bunker, the assistant cashier, "come and open this safe, or you see what your luck will be!"

Bunker declared he did not know the combination, and with that made a bold dash and escaped through the back door; but as he was flying from the scene of death he received a bullet in his left shoulder. Mr. Frank Wilcox, the junior clerk, escaped without any molestation.

The robbers then searched for the cashier's money

box, but they found nothing but a very small box half-filled with nickels. This they scattered in grim disgust over the form of the dead cashier, who lay in a pool of blood. They pursued their search a little longer, when the strange excitement of the street arrested their attention.

A fearful scene met their gaze. Dr. Wheeler, a brave and courageous gentleman who occupied rooms immediately opposite the bank building, saw what was going on, and scaring up an old shotgun, took deliberate aim at one of the mounted brigands and shot him through the heart, and Charlie Pitts, as great a curse in Texas as the James boys were in Missouri, gave one wild yell and cried as he threw up his arms:

"My God! Boys, I'm done for!" and with an awful spasm of agony he fell head foremost upon his horse's neck, dead!

The valiant Dr. Wheeler fired again, and this time Bill Chadwell received the deadly message and rolled mortally wounded from his horse. He had just strength to groan out to one of his comrades: '"Take my revolvers, keep 'em for my sake," and these were the last words of the greatest desperado and horse-thief ever raised in Minnesota.

Others now joined the fray. Mr. A. K. Manning,

Joe Hyde and George Betts obtained guns and joined in the dreadful melee. Excitement ran wild. Another of the bandits was wounded and fell from his horse, which ran riderless out of the town, but one of his companions flung him across his horse and rode away with him. At this point a Mr. J. S. Allen, a brave and highly respected citizen, turned his steps toward the bank, but he was soon arrested with the threat: "D—n you, turn back. I'll blow your brains out if you squeal."

Things had got to a horrible pass. Two of the robbers lay dead in the street, another was badly wounded, and Dr. Wheeler and Mr. Manning were both firing away with most admirable zeal.

Northfield was turned into a perfect pandemonium. An eye-witness of that awful scene says:

"It was as if hell was let loose, and men of ordinarily quiet character sprung into demons in an hour!"

Frank and Jesse James and Cole Younger, coming out of the bank, took the whole situation in in a moment, and leaped to their horses and fled from the awful scene. But quick as thought the insulted citizens of Northfield resolved on avenging themselves on these blood-thirsty cut-throats, and with all speed fifty of them mounted and set off in hot pursuit.

It was indeed "Black Thursday" in the history of that lawless brood. Two of the leaders dead and a third wounded.

The tragic raid into Minnesota did not exhaust all its dark and dread romance in the quiet town of Northfield. Over hill and dale and through forest and ravine the trail of blood was carried.

Before the Jameses could leave the town there were fifty citizens mounted and ready for the pursuit. Chadwell and Pitts lay dead in the street, but they had no time to take a last look at their cold faces! Away they sped, for there was danger in the air. And every moment of delay endangered them more and more.

Information of the murder and attempted robbery was spread far and wide; it thrilled the telegraph wires, it was borne on every breeze, it was passed from lip to lip. There was but one topic of conversation in that whole region and that was concerning the tragedy at Northfield. In less than twenty-four hours four hundred well-armed citizens had formed themselves into a compact phalanx to rid the region of these murdering, plundering scoundrels! And it must be admitted that they were more successful than all

the detective forces had ever been. Albeit they did
not capture either Frank or Jesse James.

"These detectives," said one of the hunting party,
"are always *going* to do something! They have a way
of looking awfully wise and cunning. There's mystery enough in one smart detective to run a country,
but it's about all mystery. Darn them! If they were
worth their salt, poor Haywood wouldn't be lying in
his coffin today."

"You're about right," said his companion; 'the only
way to take these men is just to *go and take them,
dead or alive!* And I, for one, don't mean to come
back till we've rid Minnesota of these shameless blacklegs!"

The tidings soon reached St Paul, and Captain
Macy, private secretary to Governor Pillsbury, offered
under the instructions of the Governor a reward of
$1,000 for each of the robbers, or $6,000 for the sur-
vivers of this band of men exceeding bold.

The bandits fled, but they found that the terrible
news was ahead of them, and every way, and ford,
and creek, was guarded by some volunteers who were
set on their capture. They came to the little village
of Shieldsville and they galloped through the long
street, firing right and left, and yelling like demons, to

secure for themselves a safe passage. On they passed
into LeSeur county. Jim Younger was bleeding well-
nigh to death and his blood trail served as a guide for
the pursuers. It is averred, but with what truth it is
impossible to tell, that Jesse James wanted to have Jim
Younger killed, to put him out of awful misery and
make their escape more sure. But this has an air of
great improbability about it. For when the Youngers
and the Jameses did part, they parted as friends, and
the Youngers consigned to their comrades the custody
of all their money and jewels, which would hardly
have been the case if so wanton and cruel a proposition had been made.

The fugitives wandered on, day after day and night
after night, until at last their jaded and wearied horses
had to be left, and for further purposes of safety they
thought it best to proceed on foot. Bill Chadwell, who
was their guide and to whom they trusted to pilot
them through a new country, was lying dead at Northfield. And they were oftentimes at their wits' end
through their ignorance of the geography of the country. They were afraid to turn lest the turn should
land them into the lap of their enemies. After six
days of this weary pilgrimage they came round by
Mankato and hoped against hope that their pursuers

were growing weary of the search; they came upon a farmhouse and begged a chicken—for they lived chiefly on green corn for a week—but they had to fly, for they heard the shouts of people who were mad with excitement, because they thought they had the fugitives almost in their grasp. They were fired upon, and both the Jameses were wounded somewhat seriously.

The day after this episode it was thought best that the company should divide. So Frank and Jesse went their way from the bottoms of the Blue Earth River, and the three Youngers and Clell Miller took another route.

We will follow now for a little the course of the weary, wounded, dispirited four. They had passed through the county of Blue Earth and were taking a westerly course into Watonwan county. They had traveled in and out a hundred and twenty-five miles since they had left Northfield, though they were but seventy-five miles away in a straight line. Their foes were fast closing round them. Their doom was sealed. They had lived on such vegetables as the field had provided. They dared not light a fire if even they had the materials. They were ragged and torn and wounded and friendless. They had made war upon

society for many long years, and now the terrible time
had come. Sheriff McDonald tracked them to a dis-
mal swamp near Madelin, and now the poor bandits
were fairly entrapped! Hundreds against four! What
could they do? But they fought to the last! A heavy
ball came crashing through Jim Younger's jaw. The
wail that broke from him was terrible, but not half as
horrible as the awful sight he presented with the lower
part of a sad face shot away. Still they fought on.
Once again a terrible cry was heard above the reports
of gun and pistol, and Clell Miller flung up his hands
and cried:

"Oh! my God, boys, I'm done! But don't give in!"

And with that the dying bandit fell against a tree,
groaned once or twice and died.

Closer and closer the terrible network drew around
the three struggling brothers. Worn and spent with
travel and hunger and fatigue, and now riddled
through and through with shots, they fought while
they could stand, and revealed that whatever faults
they had, they had at least the courage and endurance
that in a better cause would have made the world
proud of their names. What might have been fame
was now infamy.

The three boys were captured and were taken to

Madelia, and there, after months of suffering, they were arraigned for trial at the Rice County Court at Faribault. They were charged with murder. But under the counsel of their legal advisers they were persuaded to plead guilty as the only means of sparing their necks. They were sentenced to be confined in the State Penitentiary for the term of their natural lives. The iron gates in the prison of Stillwater swung back upon them in the brightness of an October morning! They are there still—wiser and perhaps on the whole happier men than they were in their wild lawless days! Who can tell?

But what of the heroes of these pages? How were Frank and Jesse faring? After leaving the Youngers in the Blue Earth River bottoms they went into a perfect wilderness, and were so completely surrounded by their pursuers that their escape seems to have been half miraculous. It is true they had had long years of experience in this direction. They had ten days of such horrible trial that one would think that, once delivered from these perils, they would never have cared to venture in these ways again. They would hide behind a tree and hear three or four citizens pass within a yard of where they stood talking, and declaring that they saw them only a moment ago. They lived on green corn and new potatoes. They could not make a fire, and they dare not if they could. They forded streams and swam rivers. They often managed by these means to cover up their tracks. At last they got out into the open country. They then ventured to buy a couple of horses, and they got a hearty meal at a poor woman's house whose husband had gone to hunt these dreadful murderers! They now lost no time, but rode all night and began to hope that all danger was passed. But in this they were mistaken! On the border of Iowa they were met by seven armed but poorly mounted men. There was a most severe contest, and Frank received an ugly wound; but their old-time skill on horseback came back to them. Three of the seven were wounded, two were killed, and the brothers escaped. After this fierce and prolonged contest, Frank and Jesse found themselves once again safe and sound in their old retreat in Jackson county.

But the robber band was broken. The Youngers no more could carry on this strange war against society, and three of the ringleaders were dead.

CHAPTER XV.

CHICAGO AND ALTON TRAIN AND THE CONCORD CAVE COACH ROBBERIES.

The next scene of the James gang's exploits was at Glendale, a lonely flag station in Lafayette county, Missouri, on the Kansas City branch of the Chicago and Alton Railway.

The male population of Glendale numbered six when the James boys took the census one evening in the late seventies, when everybody was in the town except the station agent, who was sitting outside the postoffice store.

"It's a fine night, Mr. Anderson," said one of the company.

" 'Deed it is," added the postmaster.

"But there's a storm brewing, I'm thinking," added a third, who little knew what allegorical truth there was in his prognostication.

At this point a stranger suddenly made his appearance, and tapping the somewhat astonished postmaster on the shoulder, said:

"I want you."

"What do you want?" asked the postmaster.

The new arrival did not deign to answer the question, but quietly stepped away, and said:

"Here, boys."

In a minute—nay, a moment—half a dozen rough-looking men, muffled and masked, stood by his side, armed with huge pistols and wicked-looking knives. Their pistols they held cocked in their hands. Then the leader, in a harsh, grating voice, said:

"Now, take care, make tracks out of this!"

"Where are we to go?" asked the man who had just prophesied a storm.

"To the depot," was the brief answer. And so the little company filed off to the depot. There was Mr. McIntyre, the operator and agent. His venerable mother was in a room overhead, and Mr. W. E. Bridges, assistant auditor of the Chicago and Alton Line, was taking tea with Mrs. McIntire in the room over the office.

The leader of the masked men, for there were twelve of them now at the door of the depot, sauntered lazily into the office and said:

"I want to send a message to Chicago."

"All right," said Mr. McIntyre. But before he was well aware a heavy hand was laid on his arm and he was pulled back with the astonishing announcement:

"You are my prisoner!"

In a moment the instrument was torn from its place and rendered utterly useless. The instrument was smashed.

"Now," said the leader, whose only mask was a long dark beard, "I want you to lower that green light!"

"But," said the agent, "the train will stop if I do."

"That's the alum!—precisely what we want it to do, my buck, and the sooner you obey orders the better. I will give you a minute to lower the light," said the bearded leader, at the same time thrusting a cocked pistol to the face of the agent.

The operator could see the long bright barrel of the pistol, and yielded at discretion.

The order was obeyed with the reluctance with which a conscientious man puts his hand to such work, but the agent was powerless to resist, and he obeyed the order.

Before this was done he had been asked, "Anybody upstairs? Do you hear?" and he had answered truthfully that his mother was there, and that the traveling auditor of the road and she were taking tea when he came down.

One of the robbers mounted the stairs and soon relieved Mr. Bridges of his money and a handsome gold watch. Mrs. McIntyre was almost frantic with fear for her son's safety, but was assured that he should not be harmed if he did as he was told.

The robbers now concealed themselves and waited for the train, which was now at hand.

At the moment of its arrival two of the masked robbers rushed to the cab of the locomotive and demanded the coal hammer.

"What do you want with it?" asked the engineer.

"Never do you mind! Hand it here quick, or you'll never have use for a hammer again," was the response.

The hammer was yielded and soon was brought into requisition to break open the door of the express car, which had been securely locked on the first gleam of danger by the messenger, Mr. William Grimes. The faithful custodian of the express treasures had formed the plan of hiding the gold or escaping with it. He took most of the money out of the safe and hastily deposited it in a satchel which he carried with him. He swung the safe door to, and was making for the further door of exit.

He was one moment too late! The robbers confronted him.

"Here, you!" said one of them, "give me the key of that d——d safe, and quick!"

"I will not," said Grimes; "take it if you want to!"

In a moment the faithful Grimes lay senseless on the floor from a blow from the butt end of a revolver. The safe was ransacked, the money in the satchel was taken and other valuables. The train had waited ten minutes at Glendale, but *not* for refreshments! During that brief space the sum of $35,000 to $40,000 had been stolen. The train was then ordered to proceed. The prisoners were released from the station house.

One evening shortly after the Chicago and Alton train robbery, the Concord Cave coach came rumbling along, carrying seven gentlemen and one lady. The coach had got well under the gloomy shadow of the wood, when the driver descried faintly two horsemen in the distance. He took little notice of them till they got nearer. The younger of the two suddenly cried, "Halt!"

And with that presented a pair of revolvers at the driver's head and covered the whole stage. The driver pulled up and was ordered to the door of his coach. He saw at once whom he had to deal with, and by

their peremptory manner as much as by their personal
appearance he knew the strangers to be Frank James
and one of his gang, and begged his passengers, if
they valued their lives, to yield to the highwaymen
without a moment's resistance, arguing with an irre-
sistible logic:

"You see, they'll have your money, anyhow, and if
you bother 'em they'll have your life as well as your
money."

"Come out of the stage, please," said the rider who
had first commanded the halt.

The order took the shape of the most polite request.
The passengers looked through the open windows and
saw the muzzles of two pair of revolvers, commanding
the whole line of the stage. The passengers needed
no further argument. Mr. R. S. Rountree, of the Milwaukee *Evening Wisconsin*, was wide awake to the
importance of the hour, and managed to slip his gold
watch and pocketbook under the cushion as he rose to
leave the stage. Miss Rountree, daughter of the Hon.
R. Rountree, of Lebanon, Ky., the only lady on board,
was permitted to retain her seat. After the passengers
were out and stood in single file, Frank James tossed
his rein to his companion, who covered the whole line
with his pistols, and then proceeded to search their

Planning the robbery of the Concord Cave Coach

pockets, while they were charged to hold up their hands and keep them up. There seems not to have been the first thought of resistance. How successful the raid was may be gathered from the following de-tailed

CATALOGUE OF THE SWAG.

The cash:

J. E. Craig, Jr., Lawrenceville, Ga.............$670

Hon. R. H. Rountree, Lebanon................ 55

S. W. Shelton, Calhoun, Pa................. 50

S. H. Frohlichstein, Mobile.................. 23

G. M. Parsley, Pittsburg..................... 33

G. W. Welsh, Pittsburg..................... 5

Total...............................$936

Besides this they bagged about $200 worth of jewelry. When they were through with their examination and robbery, they generously returned the railway passes and tickets that were no manner of use in the world to them. Then, with the utmost nonchalance, they proceeded to explain that they were not robbers! Oh! dear, no, nothing so vulgar! They were only moonshiners who, unduly pressed by an unreasonable government, were compelled to leave the country, and of course they could not go without money. And, therefore, though much against their principles, they were compelled to levy toll after this fashion. They were extremely sorry if they had given any undue annoyance. It might be some consolation to know that they had taken toll from the outgoing coach that very afternoon, and Mr. George Crogham, one of the owners of the celebrated cave, had contributed the handsome sum of $700.

Turning to Mr. Craig, of Georgia, Frank said he hated worse than anything to take his money, for in the late war he had fought in a Georgia regiment himself, but then he had no option.

"You know, my dear sir," said Frank, with a smile, "needs must when the devil drives."

Turning to the only lady of the party, the impertinent robber inquired her name.

"Miss Rountree, of Lebanon," said the lady, scarcely able to hide her disgust.

"Indeed!" said Frank, his face quite lighting up with a smile. "Why, then, you'll probably know some friends of mine. I have some very dear friends in Lebanon. Do you happen to know the Misses Smithers who live there?"

"Yes, sir, I do," replied Miss Rountree.

"Dear me," added Frank, "what a coincidence! Nice

girls the Smithers girls, ain't they? Real jolly girls!
No nonsense, you know, but real out and outers! I
wish you'd give my love to them when you see them.
Tell them not to be afraid, I'll make all this right."

By this time the passengers were again in the stage
and Frank ordered the driver to drive on, and as the
old stage rumbled along he shouted a farewell request
to Miss Rountree:

"Be sure and give my love to the girls!"

The old coach rumbled on to the great Mammoth
Cave; its occupants were sad and morose and gloomy,
their lightness of pocket accounting for their heaviness
of heart.

But Frank James and James Cummings, heavy of
pocket and light of heart, rode off in another direction.

CHAPTER XVI.

KILLING OF CONDUCTOR WESTFALL IN THE CHICAGO,
ROCK ISLAND AND PACIFIC TRAIN ROBBERY,
NEAR WINSTON, MO.

The train left Kansas City on time on the memorable Friday night, and all went well till it reached
Cameron, at which spot a number of the notorious
gang boarded the train. At the next station east,
Winston. the remaining members of the robber brood
entered the train. It was now dark, and the train had
not gone far out of Winston, when the murderous
work began. The bell connecting with the engine was
pulled, presumably by some affrighted passenger. The
fireman, guessing something was wrong, said to the
engineer, "Give her hell!" The engineer suddenly
turning round, became aware of two masked men with
drawn revolvers, seeming as though they were rising
right off the coals, glaring like fiends, one of whom
said in hoarse, commanding tones, "Go on, you ——

—— ——," and he instantly pulled the throttle clean out of the valve, put out the light, and escaped almost miraculously through a rain of pistol shots. He and the fireman hung on to the cowcatcher for awhile and then escaped to the woods. Meantime a dreadful work was going on in the cars. William Westfall, the conductor, was collecting tickets, when a masked man— undoubtedly the leader of the gang, Frank James— dressed in a linen duster and wearing a straw hat, followed by two others, came into the car, muttering something to the effect of "You are my prisoner, you are the man I want." Without time for a moment's reply, the quick, sharp crack of the revolver was heard and the conductor was shot. Westfall reeled against the seat and attempted to go out of the rear door of the car. But all in vain. Shot followed shot, and where the bullets struck blood oozed forth from the crimson fountain. Westfall fell dead without a word on the platform, and as the train was now slacking its pace, his lifeless body rolled to the ground. Poor McMillan, a stone mason, in the employ of the company, coming to the door of the smoking car, was shot instantly dead by one of the stray shots. A scene of indescribable tumult followed. The masked robbers went through the cars, firing their revolvers through

the roof and threatening with instant death any who
should dare to stir. The panic of suspense was awful.
Big, stout men crawled to the floor and tried to get
under the seats. Others tried to hide in the Pullman
car, where one devout old lady was heard amid all the
tumult praying aloud that the good Lord would turn
the hearts of these wicked men and spare the lives of
the passengers.

For the most part the women were much more
courageous than the men, the latter hiding their valuables in all conceivable places, utilizing the water-
cooler, the spittoons and their boots as secret hiding
places for jewelry, watches and pocketbooks, while
others held up their valuables as a sacrifice to appease
the avarice of these miserable ghouls. One poor
wretch, scared well-nigh to death, notwithstanding he
was armed, pulled out his revolver and laid it on the
window-sill, saying, "Here, anybody can have this; I
don't want it." One passenger in the Pullman car took
the precaution to hide all his money in one of the pil-
lows, which, perhaps, was the safest and wisest place
under the circumstances. The prevailing idea was that

the robbers were going through the train to plunder and murder every passenger, if need be. But this was not their purpose. To keep the passengers terror-stricken for a little time was all they wanted of them. But the real work of the robbers was going on in the baggage car, where the valuables of the express company are always kept.

The night was very warm—it was mid-July—the baggage van was in charge of Messenger C. H. Murray and Baggageman Stampes, and they had the door of the car partly open for the sake of ventilation. When the train so suddenly stopped Stampes was going to the door to see what was the matter, but he was suddenly grabbed by the legs by one of four masked men, who said, in a savage tone of voice:

"Come out, you —— of a ——, come out!"

With this Stampes was dragged to the ground and told that if he moved an inch or spoke a word he would be shot instantly dead.

Holding Stampes thus in guard, the robbers next sought for Murray, the expressman in charge. He had for a moment hidden behind some trunks. They

rushed for the door, but he had managed to slam it
to and bar it. Then they began firing at the door.
Twelve bullets were subsequently found in the door.
One went through the door and grazed Murray's
shoulder. Enraged at this delay they by means of an
ax burst open the door, yelling: "Where is that ——
—— ——?"

At this Murray rose from among the trunks and
said:

"Here I am; what do you want?"

He was grabbed, whirled round two or three times,
then struck with the butt end of a pistol, and the key
of the safe was, of course, demanded without a moment's delay.

Murray says that during their search of the safe
one of the robbers held two pistols within an inch of
his nose and his right temple and never for one moment took his awful eye off him.

The leader of the gang then pulled out a sack and
put all the money he could find into it, asking the
guarded Murray how much money there was. Murray said he didn't know.

"Then you ought to know," said the leader. "What the devil do you do here in charge without knowing? Come, now, be quick! I want all you have, every cent! And if you give me any more trouble, I'll kill you, by God!"

Murray said. "You've got everything but those silver bricks."

"Oh, d——n your silver bricks!" was the rejoinder. "You might as well give up. We have killed your conductor and engineer, and we are going to kill you, so get down on your knees. , There are twelve men in this gang, and we've got full possession of the train."

But Murray had no more to give them, and so, having soundly abused him and struck him again with the revolver, they left the cars.

It was no part of their purpose to rob the passengers. They were not of the wealthy sort; and, besides, the time wasted in going through a whole train, except under very special circumstances, largely enhances the danger. So, having secured all the safe contained, they escaped to the woods, where they left their horses.

They only secured $2,000 by this raid, and that divided among seven would not be a large fortune for each.

The conductor of the train, William Westfall, who fell a victim in the fray, shot dead without time for a dying word, his blood and brains scattered all along the smoking car and on the platform in front, was an old and widely respected conductor on the line. An opinion is somewhat current that one of the motives of the onslaught, if not the chief motive, was vengeance on Westfall. It is reported that Westfall was a conductor on the Hannibal and St. Joe Line some years ago, when the James brothers attacked and robbed a train, and that when the Pinkerton agents went in vain pursuit of the thieves, Westfall was conductor of the train and acted in the capacity of guide to the Pinkerton clan. Some years ago a half-brother of the James brothers was killed in a melee and a bombshell was thrown into the house of Mrs. Samuels, the mother of these men. It is believed that Westfall was concerned in both these acts of rough retribution, and that therefore the James brothers cherished towards him the bitterest spirit of revenge. And as the old crusader had wrought upon his shield, "I bide my time," so these border scoundrels waited for a convenient season for their revenge. However this may be, and whatever their motive was, the gang did their work most effectively.

On the evening of the 16th of July, forty-eight hours after the robbery, the following letter was found on Dog Creek bridge, but a short distance from the spot where the robbers left the train and took to their horses:

KANSAS CITY, July 12, 1881.

CHARLEY: I got your letter today, and was glad to hear you had got everything ready in time for the 15th. We will be on hand at the time. Bill will be with me. We will be on the train. Don't fear. We will be in the smoker at Winston. Have the horses and boys in good fix for the feast. We will make this joust on the night of the 16th inst. All is right here. Frank will meet us at Cameron. Look sharp and be well fixed. Have the horses well gaunted. We may have some riding to do sometime. Don't get excited, but keep cool till the right time. Willco (evidently meant for Willcott) will be on the engine. I think it best to send this to Kidder.

Yours till and through death, ALECK.

CHAPTER XVII.

DEATH OF JESSE JAMES AND SURRENDER OF HIS BROTHER FRANK ON THE MORNING OF MONDAY, APRIL 3, 1882.

Jesse James, the Missouri outlaw, before whose acts the deeds of Fra Diavolo, Dick Turpin and Shinderhannes dwindle into insignificance, was killed by a boy 20 years old, named Robert Ford, at his temporary residence on Thirteenth and Lafayette streets, St. Joseph, Mo. In the light of all moral reasoning the shooting was wholly unjustifiable, but the law was vindicated. There is little doubt that the killing was the result of a premeditated plan formed by Robert and Charles Ford. Charles had been an accomplice of Jesse James and entirely possessed his confidence. Robert, his brother, joined Jesse near Mrs. Samuels' house, mother of the James boys, and accompanied Jesse and Charles to this city, Sunday, March 23.

Jesse, his wife and two children removed from Kansas City in a wagon to St. Joseph, Mo., arriving there November 8, 1881, accompanied by Charles Ford, and rented a house on the corner of Lafayette and Twenty-first streets, where they stayed two months, when they secured the house No. 1318 Lafayette street, giving the name of Thomas Howard.

The house was a one-story cottage, painted white, with green shutters, and romantically situated on the brow of a lofty eminence east of the city, commanding a fine view of the principal portions of the city, the river and railroads, and adapted as by nature for the perilous and desperate calling of James. Just east of the house was a deep, gulch-like ravine, and beyond a broad expanse of open country, backed by a belt of timber. The house, except from the west side, can be seen for several miles. There is a large yard attached to the cottage, and a stable where Jesse had been keeping two horses. Charles and Robert Ford had been occupying one of the rooms in the rear of the dwelling, and had secretly an understanding to kill Jesse. Before Robert had joined James the latter proposed to rob the bank at Platte City. He said the Burgess murder trial would commence there soon, and his plan was, if they could get another companion, to take a view of Platte City Bank, and while arguments were being heard in the murder case, which would engage the attention of the citizens, boldly execute one of his favorite raids. Charles Ford approved of the plan and suggested his brother Robert as a companion worthy of sharing the enterprise with them. Jesse had met the boy at the latter's house, near Richmond, three years before, and consented to see him. The two men accordingly went to where Robert was and arranged to have him accompany them to Platte City. All three came to St. Joe. They remained at the house all the week. Jesse thought it best Robert should not exhibit himself on the premises, lest the presence of the three able-bodied men who were doing nothing should excite suspicion. They had fixed upon that night to go to Platte City. Ever since the boys had been with Jesse they had watched for an opportunity to shoot him, but he was always so heavily armed that it was impossible to draw a weapon without him seeing it.

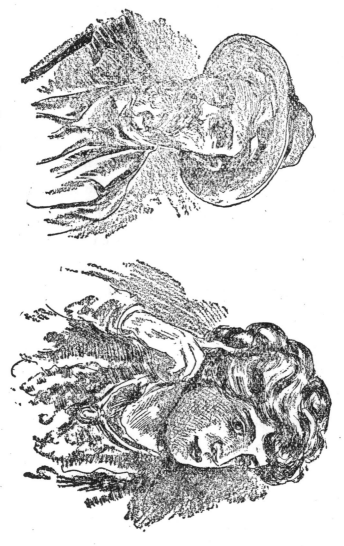

Jese James and his wife in St. Joseph, Mo.

They haa no idea of taking him alive, considering the undertaking suicidal. The opportunity they had long wished for came. Breakfast was over. Charles Ford and Jesse James had been in the stable currying the horses preparatory to their night ride. On returning to the room where Robert Ford was Jesse said: "It's an awfully hot day." He pulled off his coat and vest and tossed them on the bed. Then he said: "I guess I'll take off my pistols for fear somebody will see them if I walk in the yard." He unbuckled the belt in which he carried two 45-calibre revolvers, one a Smith & Wesson and the other a Colt, and laid them on the bed with his coat and vest. He then picked up a dusting brush, with the intention of dusting some pictures which hung on the wall. To do this he got on a chair. His back was now turned to the brothers, who silently stepped between Jesse and his revolvers, and, at a motion from Charley, both drew their guns. Robert was the quickest of the two. In one instant he had the long weapon to a level with his eye, with the muzzle no more than four feet from the back of the outlaw's head. Even in that motion, quick as thought, there was something that did not escape the acute ears of the hunted man. He made a motion as if to turn his head to ascertain the cause of that suspicious sound. But too late. A nervous pressure on the trigger, a quick flash, sharp report, and the well-directed ball crashed through the outlaw's skull.

There was no outcry, just a swaying of the body and it fell heavily back upon the carpet. The shot had been fatal, and all the bullets in the chamber of Charley's revolver, still directed at Jesse's head, could not more effectually have decided the fate of the greatest bandit and free-booter that ever figured in the pages of the country's history. The ball had entered the base of the skull and made its way out through the forehead over the left eye. It had been fired out of a Colt's 45, improved pattern, silver-mounted and pearl-handled gun, presented by the dead man to his slayer only a few days before. Mrs. James was in the kitchen when the shooting was done, divided from the room in which the bloody tragedy occurred by a dining-room. She heard the shot and, dropping her household duties, ran into the front room. She saw her husband lying on his back, and his slayers, each holding his revolver in hand, making for the fence in the rear of the house. Robert had reached the inclosure and was in the act of scaling it, when she stepped to the door and called to him, "Robert, you have done this; come back." Robert answered, "I swear to God I did not." They then returned to where she stood. Mrs. James ran to the side of her husband and lifted up his head. Life was not extinct, and, when asked if he was hurt, it seemed to her that he wanted to say something, but could not. She tried to wash away the blood that was coursing over his face from the hole in his forehead, but it seemed to her "that the blood would come faster than she could wash it away," and in her hands Jesse James died. Charles Ford explained to Mrs. James that "a pistol had accidentally gone off."

"Yes," said Mrs. James, "I guess it went off on purpose," and meanwhile Charley had gone back into the house and brought out two hats, and the two boys left the house. They went to the telegraph office and sent a message to Sheriff Timberlake, of this county, to Governor Crittenden and other officers, and then sur-

Murder of Jesse James by Bob Ford.

rendered themselves to Marshal Craig. When the
Ford boys appeared at the police station they were
told by an officer that Marshal Craig and a posse of
officers had gone in the direction of James' residence,
and they started after them and surrendered themselves. They accompanied the officers to the house,
and returned in custody of the police to the marshal's
headquarters, where they were furnished with a dinner, and about 3 o'clock were removed to the old cir-
cuit court room, where the inquest was held in the presence of an immense crowd. Mrs. James also accompanied the officers to the City Hall, having previously
left her two children, aged 7 and 3, a boy and girl, at
the house of Mrs. Lurnal, who had known the Jameses
under their assumed name of Howard ever since they
occupied the adjoining house. She was greatly affected
by the tragedy, and her heart-rending moans and ex-
pressions of grief were sorrowful evidences of the love
she bore the desperado. The report of the killing of
the notorious outlaw spread like wildfire through the
city, and, as usual, the reports assumed every variety
of form and color. Very few credited the news, how-

ever, and simply laughed at the idea that Jesse James was really the dead man. Nevertheless, the excitement ran high, and one confirming report succeeded another. Crowds of hundreds gathered at the undertaking establishment where laid the body, at the City Hall, at the courthouse, and, in fact, on every street corner, the almost incredible news constituting the sole object of conversation.

Coroner Heddens was notified and Undertaker Sidenfader instructed to remove the body to his establishment. A large crowd accompanied the coroner to the morgue, but only a few, including a reporter, were admitted. Nothing in the appearance of the remains indicated the desperate character of the man or the many bloody scenes in which he had been an actor. Only the lower part of the face, the square cheek bones, the stout, prominent chin, covered with a soft, sandy beard, and thin, firmly-closed lips, in a measure betrayed the determined will and iron courage of the dead man. A further inspection of the body revealed two large bullet holes on the right side of the breast, within three inches of the nipple, a bullet wound on the leg, and the absence of the middle finger on the left hand.

Thus ended the career of the boldest and bravest outlaw the world has ever known.

A dramatic scene was that which was enacted at the Governor's mansion in Jefferson City on October 5th, 1882. The sun was just declining as Major John N. Edwards, editor of *The Sedalia Democrat,* a life-long friend of the James boys, walked up to the front gate of the Governor's mansion. He was accompanied by a man a little above the medium height, with dark eyes and brown hair, and who walked a trifle lame. The two entered the yard in front of the Governor's residence and walked right into the office. The Governor was in at the time, and to the outsider it would appear that the whole action was a preconcerted one. Major Edwards entered the office first, and as the man behind him followed, the Major shook hands with the Governor, and then wheeled about, saying: "Governor Crittenden, allow me to introduce you to Frank James."

The Governor advanced and accepted the proffered

hand. Then Frank unbuckled his belt, and, handing it and his revolver to the Governor, he said:

"No living man but me has had hand on this revolver since 1861."

THE END.

Part Three - Editor's Conclusion

Conclusion

Thaddeus Thorndike was obviously not a scholar or historian, but rather a popular author aiming at reaching a mass audience with his sensational and adventurous account of the lives and exploits of the James Gang. Those interested in a recent scholarly history of the topic should consult William A. Settle, Jr., *Jesse James Was His Name* (1966). Another excellent work is by George Huntington, *The Story of the Northfield Bank Robbery, With an Introduction by John McGuigan* (1986). Other recent books are: John Ernst, *Jesse James* (1976), L.C. Bradley, *Jesse James* (1980), and P.W. Steele, *Jesse and Frank James: The Family History* (1987).

An annotated bibliography of the numerous books dealing with the James brothers, most of which are of a sensational nature, can be found listed in Ramon F. Adams, *Six-Guns and Saddle Leather* (1969). One work which aims to bluntly state the basic facts about the Wild West is Peter Lyon, *The Wild, Wild West: For the Discriminating Reader: A Chilling Illustrated History Presenting the Facts About A Passal of Mischievous Personages Including Joaquin Muriat, Wild Bill Hickock, Jesse James, Bat Masterson, Wyatt Earp & Billy the Kid...* (1969).

Thaddeus Thorndike's book was first published in 1909 by I. and M. Ottenheimer of Baltimore, Maryland, which published a total of nine books dealing with various aspects of the James Gang. This publication focus is an indication of the sustained and substantial interest in the James brothers' activities several decades after the demise of the group in the 1880s. Many of Ottenheimer's books were of the "dime-novel" format, and contributed to the legends surrounding the James boys. Thorndike's book appeared in such a cheap paperback format.

The book is a good example of the type of popular and sensational literature which appeared at the turn of the century and appealed to a mass audience. Its particular value is that it is an example of this type of popular literature, and, second, it demonstrates what was being published with regard to a popular topic.

Aside from the aforementioned works, which the reader may want to consult, there are a number of sources which were written by those close to the James brothers, or to their family. A general history of the Gang can be found in Homer Croy, *Jesse James Was My Neighbor* (1949). For an account by the son of Jesse James, see Jesse James, Jr., *Jesse James My Father* (1899). The autobiography of gang member Cole Younger is found in his *The Story of Cole Younger, By Himself* (1901). Frank James never published anything, according to, Stella F. James, the wife of Jesse James, Jr., for some very obvious reasons. "...indeed he had sufficient reason: though he had been acquitted of implication in a train robbery, and murder, and a payroll holdup, there were at least a dozen such incidents he could have been charged with if he had admitted participation." This and more on the James family can be found in her recently published, fascinating book, which is entitled *In the Shadow of Jesse James* (1990).

As noted earlier, numerous films have been made about Jesse James and his gang. In 1933, Jesse James, Jr. played himself and his father in "Jesse James as the Outlaw" and also in "Jesse James under the Black Flag." Every decade seems to bring with it another film about the James boys. Most notable, however, are the four films produced in 1939, 1972, 1980, and 1991.

In 1939 Darryl F. Zanuck produced "Jesse James" for Twentieth Century Fox. It starred Tyrone Power as Jesse and Henry Fonda as Frank James. Described as "a glossy re-creation" of the Jesse James story, the film was "a highy fictional and glamorized account," but "was a big hit with the public..." Filmed in Technicolor, the great success of the film led Fox to produce more Westerns, including "The Return of Frank James" in 1940. (1)

In 1972 Bruce Graham produced "The Great Northfield, Minnesota Raid" for Universal. The 1972 film contrasts sharply with the 1939 production, since it "failed to draw any mass support," and Robert Duvall's depiction of Jesse James "was a far cry from the romantic image created by Tyrone Power..." However, the film itself "was a factual recreation of true events -- more than can be said for that Twentieth Century Fox or any other accounts of the legendary Jesse James and his cohorts." (2)

In 1980 Tim Zinneman produced "The Long Riders" for United Artists. The film starred James Keach as Jesse James and his brother Stacy Keach as Frank James. The three Carradine brothers played the role of the Younger boys. The casting, hence, gave it an aspect of authenticity, using actual brothers in the major roles. The movie is widely considered by critics to be one of the last great American Westerns to have been filmed, and was also considered to have had an excellent script.

In 1991 documentary filmmaker Ron Casteel produced "The Life and Death of Jesse James," which contains new documentary information. The documentary cites a letter recently discovered at the National Archives, which sheds light on the explosion of 26 January 1875 at the James family farm. The letter was among the papers of Allan Pinkerton, head of the detective agency and later founder of the Secret Service. In the 1870s, his agency, which had once guarded Abraham Lincoln, was working for the "robbery-plagued railroads and banks." The letter in question was addressed to a lawyer, Samuel Hardwicke, a local contact for Pinkerton. According to the documentary, Pinkerton "gave detailed instructions for a raid on the farm in the hills outside Kearney." According to the film, "Pinkerton told Hardwicke: 'Above everything destroy the house...Let the men take no risk, burn the house down." Pinkerton also told him to have the raiders use "Greek Fire," a primitive type of a bomb. Instead of bringing the James Gang to an end, the bombing in 1875 brought great public sympathy for the James Brothers. The new evidence contained in the documentary film is "the first evidence that the Pinkertons conspired and then set off the explosion...It shows planning and execution of a callous and deadly act," according to the film's producer. (3)

This recent production is an indication of the continued interest in the life of Jesse James, and of the fact that the final word has not been said about him; new information and documentation can be found. Hopefully, this and future works will not only sharpen the historical image, but will also study the legendary aspects of Jesse James.

For those interested in historical sights and re-enactments, there are several possibilities available. The birthplace of Jesse James, a log cabin, is located at the James Farm Historic Site, which is near Kearney, Missouri (located near I-35, 20 miles north of Kansas City, Missouri), and contains the original furnishings. Near the site is the James Farm Museum, which maintains collections of materials which belonged to the James brothers. Here there are exhibits, as well as an audio-visual presentation. Morever, each August an historical drama is presented, *The Life and Times of Jesse James*. Not far from the site is located the Claybrook House, which belonged to the only daughter of Jesse James, Mary James Barr.

In the Mt. Olivet Cemetery, located in Kearney, Missouri, the graves of members of the James family can be found, including Jesse and his wife. On James' tombstone the inscription reads:

In Loving Remembrance of My Beloved Son

Jesse James

Died April 3, 1882

Aged 34 Years, 6 Months, 28 Days

Murdered By A Traitor And Coward Whose

Name Is Not Worthy To Appear Here.

Each September, Northfield, Minnesota, presents "The Defeat of Jesse James Days," which attracts fifty thousand people annually. In the city of Northfield, the First National Bank has been turned into an interesting historical museum, with informative displays, and books and postcards dealing with the James Gang.

Among the numerous songs about James, one of them contains the lines "Jesse James was a man, a friend to the poor/He never would see a man suffer pain..." A few stanzas from this well-known song are as follows:

Jesse had a wife to mourn all her life.
   Two children they were brave.
'Twas a dirty little coward that shot Mr. Howard
   And laid Jesse James in his grave.

It was Bob Ford, the dirty little coward,
   I wonder how does he feel,
For he ate of Jesse's bread and slept in Jesse's bed,
   Then he laid Jesse James in his grave.

Notes

Preface

1. The volume which is the source of the illustrations found at the end of Part One is J.A. Dacus, *Illustrated Lives and Adventures of Frank and Jesse James and the Younger Brothers, the Noted Western Outlaws*, (St. Louis: N.D. Thompson & Co., 1881). A special thanks to the Archives and Special Collections Department, Ohio University, for making this volume available to me, and to Professor Thomas for assistance in locating it at his University Library.

Foreword

1. *The Renville County History Book*, (Dallas, Texas: Taylor Publishing Co., 1981), p. 285. I would like to thank my father for permission to quote him in this book. The editor examined the 1916 history of Renville County, but found that his grandfather apparently made no report of his youthful encounter with the James Gang. This history, which was compiled before the First World War, was completed at a time when Frank James and Cole Younger were still alive. The only reference to the editor's grandfather is in the section on German Evangelical Lutheran Churches in Renville County. Here it notes that Albert Tolzmann was a member of the church board of the St. Johannes-Gemeinde in Renville. See Franklyn Curtiss-Wedge, *The History of Renville County, Minnesota*, (Chicago: H.C. Cooper Jr. & Co., 1916), vol. 2, p. 1273.

2. George Huntington, *Robber and Hero: The Story of the Northfield Bank Raid, With an Introduction by John McGuigan,* (St. Paul: Minnesota Historical Society, 1986), p . 59.

3. Huntington, p, 68. An interesting example of how the James Gang tricked people is recorded in a state guide to Minnesota: "Chaska once unknowingly entertained the James-Younger gang for a few days before the Northfield raid. The gang attracted considerable attention when it rode into town on fine mounts, but the men were not recognized and were invited to sit in on a poker game with Sheriff Du Toit, the local newspaper editor, and other prominent citizens." See *Minnesota: A State Guide,* (New York: The Viking Pr., 1938), p. 392. For other interesting stories pertaining to the James Gang in Minnesota, see Merle Potter, *101 Best Stories of Minnesota,* (Minneapolis: Harrison and Smith Co.,1931). For a description of the chance meeting of Henry Clay Dean with Frank James in Corydon, Iowa, in 1871 after the holdup of the local bank there, see James Lundquist, "Before Northfield Came Iowa," *Minneapolis Star Tribune,* (1 September 1991).

4. Huntington, p. xxxvii.

5. Huntington, p. xxiii.

6. Huntington, p. xxvii

7. Huntington, p. xxxi.

8. Huntington reports that the James Gang entered Minnesota at Worthington in late August, 1876 and that their next reported appearance was 5 September at Mankato. What were they doing in the meantime? "In prospecting for a favorable opening, they visited a number of places, going as far north as St. Paul and Minneapolis, and as far east as Red Wing...They took special pains to make themselves acquainted with such features of the country as would aid or hinder them in going and coming on their intended raid." In this regard, they took note of the landscape, the villages, etc. Also, they were interested in "the extent of the country population, and the nationality and character of the people." See Huntington, pp. 3-4. In regard to the latter point, the editor notes that the James Gang, on its retreat from Northfield, stopped by German Lake in Elysian Township, and then went on to the Mankato area, where they "invited themselves to breakfast at the house of a German farmer." See Hungtinton, pp. 55-57. This raises the question whether, for some reason, James sought out regions inhabited by German-Americans as places of refuge? Perhaps he might have thought that they would be recent immigrants and would not know much about him, nor be able to speak much English?

Introduction

1. *Dictionary of American Biography,* Vol. 9 (1932),
p. 585. Captain Harrison Trow of the Quantrill
Raiders described the experiences of Jesse during the
Civil War for a book published by John P. Burch.
He describes how a Union company visited his
mother's farm one day, "hanged Dr. Samuels to a
tree until he was left for dead, and seized upon Jesse,
a mere boy in the fields plowing, put a rope about his
neck and abused him harshly, pricking him with
sabers, and finally threatening him with death should
they ever hear of his giving aid or information to the
Guerrillas" (p. 131). At the same time his mothers
and sisters were thrown into prison. Not
surprisingly, shortly before they were released, both
of the James Boys had joined the Quantrill Raiders.

Trow goes on to say Jesse "had been a desperate
Guerilla: he had fought under a black flag, he had
made a name for terrible prowess along the
(Kansas/Missouri) border; he had survived dreadful
wounds; it was known that he would fight at any
hour or in any way; he could not be frightened out
from his native country; he could be neither
intimidated nor robbed, and hence the wanton war
waged upon Frank and Jesse James, and this is the
reason they became outlaws, and hence the reason
also that - outlaws as they were and proscribed in
county, or state or territory - they had more friends
than the officers who hunted them, and more
defenders than the armed men who sought to secure
their bodies, dead, or alive" (p. 256-57). See John P.

Burch, *Charles W. Quantrell: A True History of His Guerilla Warfare on the Missouri and Kansas Border During the Civil War of 1861 to 1865, As Told by Captain Harrison Trow*, (Vega, Texas: J.P. Burch, 1923).

2. Ibid; *Grolier Encyclopedia*, (1956), vol. 11/12. p. 231, and Bill O'Neal, *Encyclopedia of Western Gun-Fighters*, (Norman: University of Oklahoma Pr., 1979), p. 167.

3. Horst H. Kruse, "Myth in the Making: The James Brothers, the Bank Robbery at Northfield, Minn., and the Dime Novel," *Journal of Popular Culture*, 10(1976): 19.

4. William A. Settle, Jr., *Jesse James Was His Name*, (Lincoln: University of Nebraska Pr., 1966), pp. 76-77.

5. Settle, pp. 77-78.

6. Settle, p. 95. Also see Lawrence Boardman, "How Northfield Blasted Bandits," *St. Paul Pioneer Press*, (1 September 1946).

7. *Dictionary of American Biography,* Vol. 9, p. 585.

8. Huntington, p. xix; *Grolier Encyclopedia,* (1956), vol. 11/12, p. 231; O'Neal, p. 167; and Mark Peterson, "A Century After His Death, Jesse James

Still Good Copy," *Minneapolis Tribune*, (4 April 1982).

9. The book by Stevens was his *The James Boys in Minnesota,* (New York: Wide Awake Library, 1882). The work by Huntington was reprinted in 1986 by the Minnesota Historical Society. Aside from being available from the Society, it is also available at the Northfield Bank in Northfield, Minnesota.

10. Huntington, pp. xxxii.

11. See Burch/Trow, p. 263. Trow told Burch that he felt that it was the Civil War which had made the James Boys Guerillas, and that the persecution of their family had made them outlaws. After the war Trow said that the former guerillas had a difficult time, which caused some to keep their weapons. "Some were killed because of the terrible reknown won in the four years' war; some were forced to hide themselves in the unknown of the outlying territories, and some were persecuted and driven into desperate defiance and resistance because they were humble and intrepid. To this latter class the Jameses and Youngers belonged" (p. 253). According to a sympathetic Trow, the Jameses could not make the transition to civilian life after the war: "They were not permitted so to do, try how they would, and as hard and as patiently" (p. 253). Trow provides insight into how the former guerillas viewed post-war life: "The peaceful pursuits of life were denied them. The law which should have protected them was overriden.

Indeed, there was no law. The courts were instruments of plunder. The civil officers were cutthroats. Instead of a legal process, there was a vigilante committee...Some Confederate soldiers dared not return home and many Guerillas fled the country" (p. 261).

12. Settle, p. 201.

13. Huntington, p. xxxii.

14. Readers might be interested in comparing and contrasting some of the colorful individuals from the Wild West era. For example, an interesting contrast to Jesse James (1847-82) would be Buffalo Bill Cody (1846-1917). For further information on him see William Roba, ed., *Buffalo Bill, the King of the Border Men,* (Quad-Cities: Hesperian Press, 1987). Roba cites the following contemporary account of the border war in Kansas/Missouri, which gave rise to individuals as different as James and Buffalo Bill. The account states, "The cruel strife of the border can never be forgotten. Those were tragic days, the very remembrance of which comes like a dream of sorrow and desolation of soul. It is well that such terrible times have passed away, for to those who were exposed to the fury of that tidal-wave of passion, which swept over the fair border-land, physical existence must have been a wheel of pain" (p. 90).

Conclusion

1. James Robert Parish and Michael R. Pitts, *The Great Western Pictures*, (Metuchen, New Jersey: Scarecrow Pr., 1976), pp. 162-63.

2. Parish and Pitts, p. 121. An interesting study in itself would be the image of Jesse James as reflected in film, together with an analysis of the public reception of these films. For a list of the films dealing with the James and Younger brothers, see Joe Hembus, *Western-Geschichte 1540 bis 1894: Chronologie/Mythologie/Filmographie*, (Muenchen: Hanser, 1979), pp. 482-83, 547-49.

3. See "Conspiracy Behind Deadly Explosion at Jesse James Farm," *The Mankato, Minnesota Free Press*, (1 July 1991).

About the Editor

Don Heinrich Tolzmann is Senior Librarian and Director of the German-American Studies Program at the University of Cincinnati. He has authored numerous books dealing with various aspects of German-American history, literature, and culture. His interest in Jesse James derives from his grandfather, Albert Tolzmann, whose path crossed that of the James Gang in 1876.